Zong!

Also by m. nourbeSe philip

Poetry
Thorns
Salmon Courage
She Tries Her Tongue; Her Silence Softly Breaks

Fiction
Harriet's Daughter
Looking for Livingstone: An Odyssey of Silence

Plays
The Redemption of Al Bumen (A Morality Play)
Harriet's Daughter (stage adaptation)
Coups and Calypsos

Nonfiction
Frontiers: Essays and Writings on Racism and Culture
Showing Grit: Showboating North of the 44th Parallel
A Genealogy of Resistance and Other Essays
BlanK: Essays & Interviews

Zong!

As told to the author by
SETAEY ADAMU BOATENG

by m. nourbeSe philip

GRAYWOLF PRESS

First published by Wesleyan University Press (USA) and Mercury (Canada), 2008. This edition first published by Silver Press (UK), 2023.

Published by Graywolf Press
212 Third Avenue North, Suite 485
Minneapolis, Minnesota 55401

www.graywolfpress.org

Published in the United States of America

ISBN 978-1-64445-304-9 (paperback)
ISBN 978-1-64445-305-6 (ebook)

2 4 6 8 9 7 5 3 1
First Graywolf Printing, 2024

Library of Congress Control Number: 2024935295

Cover design: Joss MacLennan and Denise Maxwell

Cover art: Kevin Adonis Browne

For Olokun and all the other water deities,
for the Ancestors,
for those who lost their names,
&
for Kudakwashe.

For the island without which
nothing.

Though they go mad they shall be sane,
Though they sink through the sea they shall rise again . . .

DYLAN THOMAS, *And Death Shall Have No Dominion*

The time is out of joint. O cursèd spite
That ever I was born to set it right!

SHAKESPEARE, *Hamlet*

Contents

Preface, or Late but on Time

This, the fifteenth anniversary edition of *Zong! As told to the author by Setaey Adamu Boateng,*[1] continues a journey into the unknown, the incomplete and the unfinished, generated by the work itself and its performances. I have always believed—indeed, have always known—that *Zong!*, although complete (hence its publication fifteen years ago), was unfinished, in the sense that the world, while complete, remains infinitely unfinished, and that we, each in our own individual and collective ways, are continually working to complete it. To my mind, the conundrum, complete yet unfinished, or complete in its unfinishedness, approximates an Ifá *odu*[2] or a Zen *koan*.[3]

These past fifteen years of journeying with *Zong!* have taught me many things, the most important of which is how to read the text aloud. While I always understood that there was significance to the spaces within the text, I did not understand how to honour them in a reading. Did they work like rests in music, for instance? Should I be counting them? In the very early years after publication, I would sometimes practice walking and reading the text aloud: on one occasion as I walked in the woods at a convent where I was for a solo writing retreat, I recall hearing the sound of a plane overhead during one of the gaps and sensed "something." Nothing more than "something." Was it, perhaps, the interruption of the held silence by the plane that sharpened and emphasized it?

It was not until 2012, however, some four years after *Zong!*'s publication, and the first year of the annual *Zong!* durational readings,[4] that I recognized the need for the collective voicing of the text. I also came to realize that the idea and model for this collective sounding had been laid down some two decades earlier in *She Tries Her Tongue; Her Silence Softly Breaks.*[5] "She," "the many-voiced one of one voice,"[6] would surface in the many and varied discourses within that work, which opened the ground for a poetics of polyvocality, as well as a poetics of the fragment. These ideas, alongside the fecund S/silence[7] of *Looking for Livingstone: An Odyssey of Silence,*[8] would cast a long shadow towards the future materialization of *Zong!* It was, however, through the process of the reissue of these two earlier works within the past fifteen years, in 2015 and 2018 respectively, that I developed a clearer understanding of how those works are formally foundational to *Zong!* and how they haunt the text in other ways.

She Tries Her Tongue begins the exploration and mapping of the mine-filled terrain, circumscribed by the colonially-imposed, in-the-beginning word, the father tongue (in this particular case, English), and the many silences of the mother tongues of the autochthonous, the indigene, the enslaved, and the indentured.

> English
> is my mother tongue.
> A mother tongue is not.
> not a foreign lan lan lang
> language
> l/anguish
>   anguish
> —a foreign anguish
>
> English is
> my father tongue.
> A father tongue is
> a foreign language,
> therefore English is
> a foreign language
> not a mother tongue[9]

This exploration, which would culminate in *Zong!*, is best summed up by one of my journal entries from the mid-1980s in which I grapple with an idea that many other writers and scholars have discussed—that of the "social barbarism" that underpins all art. Literature, including poetry and the lyric, which were an integral part of my colonial education, was no exception to this.

Notes from a working journal
(Ms. *She Tries Her Tongue; Her Silence Softly Breaks*—a work-in-progress):

To take the poem one step further and re-embed it, re-encrust it within its context—to put it back in the mire of its origins. So in "Discourse on the Logic of Language," the poem is sculpted out of the colonial experience—exploitation of peoples, destruction of mother tongues—to become "a work of art"—objective and, according to the canon of Literature, universal. The next step, for me, was to de-universalize it—make it specific and particular once again. Eliot talked of the objective correlative—the arousal in the reader of the exact emotion the poet felt as he wrote.[10] This assumes the existence of certain universal values that would or could prompt the reader to share with the writer his emotions. This assumption is never articulated and the so-called universal values were really a cover for imperialistic modes of thought and ways of acting upon the world. The patterns of culture, the images, the forms of thinking, the Literature that were being imposed around the world on different peoples were very specific to a very specific culture (Western/European), and a very specific class within that culture—they were however propounded as universal. So the little Black girl in the West Indies was supposed to conjure up the same feeling that Eliot had when he wrote of fogs and cats and Prufrock.

In "Discourse," by cramping the space traditionally given the poem itself, by forcing it to share its space with something else—an extended image about women, words, language, and silence; with the edicts that established the parameters of silence for the African in the New World; by giving more space to the descriptions of the physiology of speech, the scientific legacy of racism we have inherited, and by questioning the tongue as organ and concept, poetry is put in its place—both in terms of it taking a less elevated position—moving from centre stage and page and putting it back where it belongs, and locating it in a particular historic sequence of events (each reading of such a poem could become a mine drama). The canon of objectivity and universality is shifted—I hope permanently disturbed.

She Tries Her Tongue would enter the hallucinatory landscape of the colonized under which roil the missing, the erased, the forgotten, the disremembered, and the unremembered, the removed tongues which were "hung on high . . . so that all may see and tremble."[11]

It may be helpful to see *She Tries Her Tongue* as a first statement—the thesis, if you will—in a dialectical process, but a destabilized thesis—an unthesis or anti-thesis—since what it was proposing, if poetry could be said to propose anything at all, was that the Caribbean, like the so-called New World, was a scene of massive interruptions and disruptions, where many discourses crush and grind against each other, much like tectonic plates do and, as in the case of the Caribbean, more often than not fatally. The autochthonous, the European, the African, the Asian—all these peoples and cultures would collide, coming up hard against each other, even as one, the European, bearing the mantle of enlightenment, rationality, and superiority enforced their ways on all others to establish a racial hierarchy with the African at the bottom. To attempt to "write" that experience in a way that would do justice to it meant that the writing could not echo or represent the top-down, left-to-right way in which we were educated to read and how we were and are taught to function, hence the attempt in "Discourse on the Logic of Language" to occupy the stage that is the page spatially. In that poem margins would be drafted into use, and reading the poem would require the physical effort of turning the book sideways to engage with the woman's story.

As with "Discourse," most of the poems that comprise *She Tries Her Tongue* do not necessarily have to begin at the in-the-beginning beginning on the page—all beginnings being necessarily arbitrary, and for far too many of us beyond reach, ever retreating. To my mind, therefore, to order the experience of the Caribbean in a logical, linear way would be to do it a second violence. All the inherent and impossible contradictions that make up the colonized experience and the experience of the colonized—"English/is my mother tongue . . . is/my father tongue"—needed to be on display. That which Eliot's objective correlative would have excised—the brutal history of empire, conquest, and enslavement—needed to be reimagined (from our perspective, that is) and restaged.

On its first publication, *She Tries Her Tongue* was described by many as post-modernist, and, later in its life, the book was included alongside the work of language poets. To the former categorization, I replied that *She Tries Her Tongue* could only be post-modernist if it was understood that the Caribbean was post-modernist long before the term was coined, citing examples such as code switching and bricolage that were and are integral to the culture. The response to this comment was usually silence. While I concurred with the premise of the language poets that language was not transparent, the origins of my concern with language were very different from theirs, as was the terrain I worked: the language poets were, after all, descendants of the white, colonial, settler culture for whom English, transparent or not, was a given. As I wrote in the essay "The Absence of Writing or How I Almost Became a Spy," which accompanies *She Tries Her Tongue*, "The paradox at the heart of the acquisition of this language (English) is that the African learned both to speak and be dumb at the same time, to give voice to the experience and i-mage, yet remain silent."[12] My concern with these labels was that if you *only* saw *She Tries Her Tongue* as post-modernist or language poetry, then you missed what was intensely local and specific to the Caribbean and Afro-Caribbean thought in particular, in the work. Indeed, the determination to shoehorn *She Tries Her Tongue* into Western, Northern, or European theoretical modalities was and is a continuation of the colonial approach.

***

As a poet and writer, the interrogation of language became the only way into the abominable physical, psychic, and spiritual wasteland that colonialism leaves in its wake. I discovered and confronted my profound and lasting distrust of language, this language that I had come to love through the Anglican liturgy of the *Book of Common Prayer*, as well as on the streets of Port of Spain, Trinidad: "this strange wonderful you tink it easy jive ass kickass massa day done Chagaramus is we own ole mass pretty mass pansweet language";[13] "this chattel language/babu english/slave idiom/nigger vernacular/coolie pidgin/wog pronunciation . . . this lingua franca/arrrrrrrrrgot of a blasted soul."[14] There appeared no way out, since the contamination had spread through the language itself, though it has never been seen to be contaminated or tainted by its centuries-long history of empire and colonialism.[15] This has always surprised me. For my part, I embraced the distrust and the love simultaneously. Like familiars they have been and are with me always as a writer: "I feel the loss of a tongue as if it were yesterday. I feel my dumbness but cling to it. Do not want to let it go. Feel the refusal to fashion my mouth where a rape takes place every time I speak English, around these beautifully shaped predator syllables."[16]

She Tries Her Tongue, the title poem, and also the last poem of the collection, ends with the words "pure utterance," absent a period or ellipsis, suggesting a longing for something beyond words. As if the poem itself acknowledges its own incompletion, an unfinished quality resonant with the ongoing ruptures endemic to colonial societies. *Zong!* would continue this idea of incompletion, and the pure utterance of *She Tries Her Tongue* would fully manifest in the explosion and fragmentation of language into sound in *Zong!*, particularly in the section *Ferrum*. "The Absence of Writing or How I Almost Became a Spy," the essay which accompanies and ends *She Tries Her Tongue*, would become a blueprint of sorts for my examination and exploration of language: "Essentially . . . what the African would do is use a foreign language expressive of an alien experiential life . . . (a language which) would, eventually, become her only language, her only tool to create and express i-mages about herself and her life experiences, past, present and future."[17]

As a writer born into and shaped by a colonial language within a colonial context, the Caribbean, and who continues to write within another colonial geography, Canada—places I call forensic landscapes, scenes of great crimes carried out under colour of law—the essay became an important tool for me to make an argument; in doing so, I am relieved of the need to take a position or sides in a poem—"and english is/my mother tongue/is/my father tongue"[18]—the contradictions remaining ever alive. This practice of using the essay almost as a way to siphon off the impulse to argument, logic and reason would continue into *Zong!* and emerge in *Notanda*, in which I trouble myself and the poem with how to unmake meaning and how to not-tell the story that couldn't be told yet had to be told.

It was on completion of *She Tries Her Tongue* that I first began to sense that the work needed completion outside of the written text. At first I tended only to read aloud those poems that supported the individual voice, which appear at the beginning of the book. As time went on, I would often ask students to "help me" read "Discourse," and on one occasion when asked to read "Universal Grammar," another of the multi-voiced poems, I heard myself say: " I will, if you read it with me." That is to say I became aware that the text needed a polyvocal rendering for completion, which I attributed (albeit tentatively) to a certain Caribbean aesthetic of performance. I began to associate polyvocality with traditions within African cultures of the Caribbean, and I sensed also that it was connected to women's lives and their hidden cultures.

Before these ideas could be more fully realized, as they would be in *Zong!*, the concern with language at the micro level would lead me into the many silences of *Looking for Livingstone*. Told from the perspective of the protagonist, known only as the Traveller, whose journey takes her through time over the age of the universe, *Looking for Livingstone* continues the formal engagement with the colonial script, imitating the discursive and writerly practices of the colonizer by using letters and journal entries, which recount meetings with strange tribes, the competition between explorers and the lust for recognition and fame. The Traveller seeks the source of her silence, much like the great explorers in Africa sought the source of the Nile, and along the way, like an efficient, colonial functionary, she recounts her encounters with previously unknown clans, each of which bears a name that is an anagram of the word "silence." The Ecnelis, for example, "tell of how God, feeling bored, came down to earth one day in the shape and form of a man and offered a choice to the first person he saw—a poor peasant: the word of God or silence."[19] I was attempting with this conceit to limn the tension between silence and Silence, the former representing the silencing that is integral to the colonizing project, while the latter approximated a type of paradisal imaginary of precolonial eras in which "the Cesliens had kept and cherished their Silence—given up the word and kept their Silence. They were the richer for it. None of their silence was on display in the Museum of Silence."[20]

In its exploration of the idea of S/silence and its inherent tensions, *Looking for Livingstone* could be considered the antithesis of an already unstable thesis, *She Tries Her Tongue*. The word counterpoint might, however, be more appropriate, given its connection to music and sound; a sonic counterpoint, albeit silenced, to the contaminated word.

As with *She Tries Her Tongue*, *Looking for Livingstone* also ends without a period. The Traveller surrenders "to the SILENCE within," but not before she meets, converses, and argues with the über-explorer David Livingstone, whom she identifies with the source of her silence. When he dismisses the possibility that Silence, like a waterfall or a river, could be discovered, she insists that she has "mapped and measured (her) own Silence to the last millimetre." As with *She Tries Her Tongue*, there is also a paratext, an "Author's Note" that engages with the issue of archival accuracy vis-à-vis the testimony of the original informant. Both these texts are held fast by the search for meaning within colonial geographies, which will reappear in *Zong!* some two decades later.

***

On November 29, 1781, a massacre by drowning would begin on board the slave ship *Zong*. It continued for ten days, at the end of which some 150 Africans had been thrown overboard. The explicit reason for this atrocity was to allow the owners of the ship to collect insurance monies, as was legally permitted at the time. In *Zong!*'s attempt to make meaning mean—something, anything—in the face of the murder; in the text's acceptance, even embrace, of the absence of meaning; in its commitment to exploding the word to find the silences within; and in its recognition that silence is not always an absence, a site of erasure and destruction, but can be present in its presence as Silence, the work synthesizes the ideas, impulses, and latent energies of the two earlier works. It limps along with Esu and Legba, African gods of the crossroads; stuttering and growling, it howls, all the while holding the erased and forgotten close—"the smallest cell/remembers/a sound . . . a secret order/among syllables/Leg/ba . . ."[21]

I have always understood *Zong!* to be hauntological: the haunting, however, is not only by "generations of skulls and spirits," as mentioned in *Notanda*,[22] but also by these two works, *She Tries Her Tongue* and *Looking for Livingstone*, its progenitors, whose bones have become the formal underpinning that structures the text—the word of *She Tries Her Tongue* tied to, constrained and shaped by the S/silences of *Looking for Livingstone*. In *Zong!*, however, the law, in particular the laws of empire that always "justif(ied) the could . . . (and) the authorize,"[23] would simultaneously provide the cladding for this structure and expose the law's contradictions: "suppose the law not/—a crime/suppose the law a loss."[24]

These three works, *She Tries Her Tongue*, *Looking for Livingstone*, and *Zong!* comprise a synergistic trinity, a poetic triangulation of formally reparative poetics, by which I mean that their formal properties are an essential aspect of the repair the poetics attempts. This triangulation is an uncanny echo of the formal structure at work within *Zong!*—a structure which, in approaching the geometrical, becomes architectural. Although described in *Notanda*, the organizational structure bears repeating here: in abutting lines each letter, word, phrase, or fragment thereof positions itself so that it breathes into the space above created by the words, phrases, or fragments immediately on either side of it in the line above, thus forming a triangular relationship. In other words, no word, phrase, or fragment can sit directly below another in abutting lines. It is this organizational and formal principle which lends the text its particular and, at times, peculiar shape and structure, and which has also been described as a form of spiritual architecture.[25] In turn this formal, ordering principle based on the triangle becomes an uncanny, spatial, and figurative echo of the Triangular Trade, more commonly known as the transatlantic trade in African slaves, the legacy of which is ongoing.[26]

The loosely applied dialectical model provided me a way of looking at the creation of the earlier works over time, along with their ideas, the foreshadowing of *Zong!*, as well as its backward haunting of those two earlier texts. Not so much a synthesis of those earlier works as an expression of a fluid and linguistic symbiosis, *Zong!* is constantly navigating between the desire for the "pure utterance" that arises from the contaminated, wounded, colonized wor(l)d of *She Tries Her Tongue* and the Silence that awaits the surrender (of the very same mutilated word, perhaps) of *Looking for Livingstone*. The duality of the symbiosis is, however, short-lived, given the triangulating third factor that *Zong!* introduces—the law, simultaneously everywhere, nowhere, everywhere, always. The law, indispensable midwife to the birth of these forensic histories whose legacies we live with. I like to think that in its fluidity, in its stuttering and shuddering (diss)fluency,[27] *Zong!* more closely approximates the Brathwaitian idea of tidalectics, a word carrying in sound and orthography the idea of the dialectical process, as well as the tidal currents of an "exaquaed"[28] history: how it doing we and how we doing it back.[29]

The first collective, durational reading of *Zong!* was held in the spring of 2012, and we, neophytes all, waded into it with nervous trepidation, but were held in thrall for several hours by a sonic landscape of voices, which was at times cacophonous, at others synchronous. Inexplicably voices would cohere into homophonic unison, as everyone arrived at the same word at the same time, and, just as inexplicably that unison would shatter into individual voices skittering and scattering around each other in time and space. Over the years I would come to understand that the soundscape created by these readings, not to mention their timing, are akin to the "tunnel of sound" created by the Afro-Colombian funerary ritual, the *lumbalu,* practiced by the African-descended residents of Palenque, Colombia.[30] At times, especially as the evening wore on and one grew tired, you could, often would, hook yourself to a voice, following it wherever it led, which seemed to ease the weariness: "es es/oh/es/oh oh/es es"[31] ssssounding the sibilance somewhere between ga(s)p and gap—where live the missing—the sound of . . . That first durational reading of *Zong!* repeats each year sometime between November 29th, the day the massacre began, and the ten days following, during which it continued. At each reading a winnowing of participants occurs as evening becomes night and night becomes early morning—a winnowing that is an eerie reminder of the attrition through death of the actual slave voyage (hence the need for insurance of the "cargo"). And always by fo-day morning,[32] there are always only a few of us left to bring closure to the un-telling, the long song of welcome.

Driven by the desire to offer a corrective to the compulsive terror of the slave ship, I introduced the idea of the "Protocols of Care" as a way to guide us through the long and at times difficult durational readings. Care as attention—close and loving attention—is bound up in creative acts, and as poets we care for and attend to language, tending to its needs and its demands. Indeed, I would argue that in this role of caring for language, poets execute the essential function of quality control.[33]

That is what we do as poets: we care for language and the wonderfully difficult work it does and in caring for language, we care for others, for their lives, filled with wonder, heartache, tragedy and trauma. We care for language, this thing that makes us being-human in ways those enslaved Africans on board the *Zong* were not cared for and were seen as so much "cargo" to be dispensed with. *Zong!* is a deep and profound expression of care for them, such as they did not find at the end of their lives on board the *Zong*.[34]

The Protocols mean simply that all are welcome; that there are no expectations, even to read; that one could just listen, for instance; that one could sit, stand, or lie. The Protocols remind us all, that care is present always as we reach for—attempt a corrective—trying to right the disjointed time way, way too late, but right on time for those who were considered dispensable; right on time for memory and for history, polluted as it is; and right on time for the word and its echo S/silence.

While in the process of composing *Zong!* I became aware that I wanted to contaminate the reader, or to create the possibility for such contamination to take place. The text would offer the choice between reading for legibility and meaning, thereby allowing the reader to enter the horror and profanity of the ten-day massacre, and refusing or (un)reading the story, which would leave the carnage illegible. Increasing the fragmentation of the text, which over time becomes progressively illegible, to be read as pure sound, would become part of the formal strategy I used to achieve this end. The contamination I speak of is also entangled in the idea that language itself, in this case English, is contaminated by its history of empire and colonialism, as are we for whom it is incestuously both mother and father tongue: "in my mother's mouth/shall I/use/the father's tongue/cohabit in strange/mother/incestuous words."[35] Whether we embrace legibility or resist meaning, however, we, including the victimized, are all contaminated—*ab initio*. "There are no degrees of innocence," as George Lamming writes. "To be innocent is to be eternally dead."[36] Hence the need for care of and attention to our disastrously and increasingly cataclysmic world and ourselves as its caretakers and attendants.

In these fifteen years I have come to understand that *the* most important activity happening on the page in *Zong!* is happening in the space, the white space between—between word and syllable, word and word, word and phrase; between vocable and grapheme, grapheme and morpheme; between phoneme and phrase; between the ga(s)p, and the gap it embraces—that space of the unknown and the unfinished. It is "not the words," I wrote in my journal— "it's the gaps, the spaces, the break, the rests and what happens there—that is where the energy lies, where the work begins and doesn't end—it's where the poem happens. In the break!"[37] The space I call the space of potentiality and possibility.[38] The space which those early ancestors of ours entered, not knowing that they were, indeed, and most surely, the tip of the spear of the future, sent as fevered fragments from an overdue past, bearing ways of knowing and of organization; carrying spiritual technologies, including the techniques of bending sound and blacksmithing the in-the-beginning word into "a present biblical with anticipation";[39] transforming the "oath, moan, mutter, chant and ululation"[40] of the hold and the plantation into chariots swinging low,[41] redemption songs,[42] and "Haiti, I'm sorry";[43] not to mention "de bunning and de bunning" of erstwhile oppressors.[44] Late but on time and in time.

> and always
> > the gap
> within
> > the ga(s)p
> space of
> > is
> possible
> > potent
> shall
> > Silence without
> no
>
> > > > > > > thing   is

The poem's trajectory from page to performance led to the formation of the *Zong!* Quartet, comprising myself and three musicians.[45] In the early years following publication we performed excerpts from *Zong!* improvisationally in and around Toronto. The long-standing burden of a certain hypervigilance transformed into an ability to be aware at all times of what each person was doing, which was strangely liberating. I came to a better and deeper understanding of the inherently improvisatory nature of *Zong!*, its complete (in)completeness, its unfinished (in)finitude riffing in and on the gap in the ga(s)p.

In these fifteen years I have also learnt that there is a deep spiritual technology at work within the text—a text which I have come to describe as pneumatic. The organizational principle at work in *Zong!* (described above in the context of triangulation), requires that each word or fragment be so placed that it can breathe into the space created above it. Through this process the text is allowed to breathe, to become pneumatic—most visible in the sections *Sal*, *Ventus*, *Ratio*, and *Ferrum*—in which the rags, pieces, and fragments of time and text, the scraps of meaning, must each breathe into the space above. "The text must breathe and live in the breaths of those who died and for whom we now breathe. In our reading of the text, which can be said to be arranged pneumatically, we are carrying out the act of breathing on behalf of those who could not breathe at an earlier time."[46] This pneumatic action, in turn, allows—creates a space for the reader to participate in this function of the work, which through the form itself, its bodily enactment and re-enactment by the reader, becomes not so much reparative, since what has happened is beyond repair, but an equation of love, care, and attention balancing between Then and Now. Hence, the transformation—dare I say the transubstantiation?—of the text into a pneumatic text, breathing on behalf of those who were thrown overboard the *Zong*. As the form structures itself around the breath-spaces, each of which is grounded in a potentiality shaped and defined by care and attention across and within time, the text then opens itself to becoming spiritually reparative on both sides of the time divide—for those who couldn't breathe as well as for the reader. This repair extends to the text itself, which is also constantly restoring and repairing itself, thus continuing the threefold pattern. Like breath itself, *pneuma*, contained and complete in the infinite finiteness of each inhale and exhale, the text—the spirit in the text and of the text—is ongoing, never finished.

Within the long shudder that is *Zong!*, I do consider this conversion, from textual matter into *pneuma*, on behalf of those who were deprived of breath, as a response to that earlier and profoundly tragic conversion of a similar transubstantial nature—that of human being into thing, enacted by the law. Indeed, it is more than a response, for it ushers in a phenomenological state that refuses and eschews, perhaps even exceeds the binary of a response held hostage by the logic of reason. It echoes the refusal of *She Tries*, described above, to repeat and represent the top-down left-to-right approach to the maelstrom created by empire and its benighted progeny, colonialism. It also incorporates, literally, within the body of the text, the many-voiced silences of *She Tries*—the ga(s)ps of the drowned, as well as the infinite Silence to which the Traveller surrendered in *Looking for Livingstone*. In allowing us, through the text, to breathe today for those who could not at an earlier time, the text allows time itself to collapse in and on itself. It resists chronological time—we are late—by several centuries, but right on time.

This pneumatic function is, I believe, but an alternate manifesting of the whoop, the holler, the shout, and the Doption of the Spiritual Baptists,[47] all of which are sounded in community—"the many voiced one of one voice"—even as its visual representation on the page gestures towards the Glissantian poetics of relation.[48] Self and Other—each word simultaneously resting and floating in relation to—the space above, the space below, the wor(l)d to the left, and the wor(l)d to the right. That space, the ga(s)p between, can also be construed as the space where spirit exists—some call this the space of conjure,[49] which in the Caribbean context would be described as High Science,[50] an elevated level of the practice of obeah.[51] I prefer to think of it as the domain of Esu, god of the crossroads where all and anything is possible—or not—and whose associative colour is black. The crossroads of existence where "i n i"[52] can manifest moment to breath-filled moment.

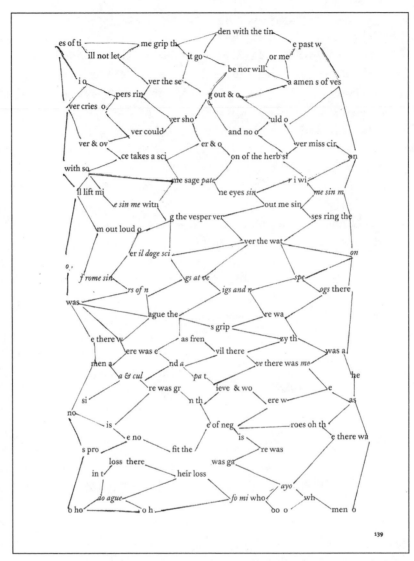

The ExtraOrdinary Fragmentary of Relation

Regarding *Zong!*, my concern with structure goes beyond the formal demands of poetry and is imbricated in the history of empire and colonialism, with which the three works engage: "Form is of great importance and significance to me as a poet and *Zong!* is a work of great formal strength, a quality that was and is necessary to meet the powerful centrifugal—Césaire refers to it as volcanic—force of the transatlantic trade in Africans (I would include the Arab trade as well)."[53] In other words, the "formal strength and rigour of the text are necessary to meet the ferocity and the cataclysm that was the Maafa.[54] You can't meet what that experience meant and survive it without having inner societal structures to meet it. Without having a rigour and a formal strength."[55] Hence my insistence on the necessity to attend to the structural underpinnings of the text, which carry the weight of memory and of history, as well as the unassuaged, ongoing loss.

While material and monetary reparations for this loss are necessary, if for no other reason than the fact that the capitalist economies and cultures we live in were created in large part from the profits of slavery and colonialism, and that reparative justice requires it, there are certain kinds of repair that only we, descendants of the Maafa, the transatlantic trade in enslaved Africans, can offer ourselves. The "we" is linked to the idea and concept of the i n i that Rasta culture embodies. It is the Glissantian "we" embedded in the poetics of relation. It is the "we" that *Zong!* attempts and tempts even in the mayhem of the slave ship. We have been encouraged to believe that the law, and consequent monetary compensation, is the most, if not the only effective way of repairing historical damage. But what if that damage were beyond repair? By the law? What then of extra-legal forms of repair and reparations, which exceed the law and cannot be caught by it? That perhaps is the domain of the artist—the storytellers, griots and griottes, the musicians and poets—those who have been called and answer the need for repair of the spirit and of being.

When I perform *Zong!*, or rather when *Zong!* performs me—this too I have learnt—I out myself as something that I am still not able to name, despite the existence of words in my culture of origin that approximate what the engagement gestures towards—Obeah woman, Shouter or Spiritual Baptist,[56] *Okyeame*[57]—or, perhaps, simply, poet, articulating one of the most ancient functions of poetry—the reciting of spells and the channeling of otherworldly forces. With the exception of "poet," I am not qualified to describe myself by any of those other terms, and I use the metaphor of "outing" because under colonial rule within my own Caribbean cultural background, non-Christian practices were abjured by the middle and aspiring lower-middle-class families such as my own. Anything that openly or too closely approximated African spiritual practices was considered evil, disparaged, and dismissed. Despite the overwhelming presence of Africa in rhythm, gesture, language, sound, and spirit. And yet and yet . . . *Zong!* "claims/ . . . maims/and claims again"[58] as the text opens itself to me . . . and to those willing to enter the work. It may simply be that in the gap within the ga(s)p—the space of breath between—the "I" surrenders to become akin to the i n i of our Rasta bredren and sistren, while simultaneously bearing witness to the necessity of the relational. I see this as the fulfilment in performance of the abdication of the authorial voice I embraced and described in *Notanda*.[59]

The shift from writing on my beloved, electronic typewriter to the computer resulted in a lasting and profound sense of destabilization—I have never felt as in control of the physical process of writing on the computer as I did on the older technology. I know, however, that the digital technology that so destabilizes was essential to the composition of *Zong!* As recounted in *Notanda*, the *Ebọra* section would not exist were it not for the computer and its "glitches." This same technology would allow us to stage the first online version of the annual, durational reading of *Zong!* during the pandemic—*Zong! Global* 2020. For ten days an international group of sixty-eight poets, scholars, and artists, representing different countries and ancestral lands around the world, took turns reading the *Zong!* text. In 2021 this was rebroadcast as part of the 24-hour livestream *RvrrbOraShuns*, featuring presentations and talks related to the unsanctioned mistranslation of *Zong!* in 2021.[60] Digital technology made all this possible.

Since publication in 2008, *Zong!* has been described as conceptual poetry, constraint poetry, erasure poetry, and generally placed within the category of avant-garde or experimental poetry. Although I understand how and why these labels apply, I find myself shifting uneasily as I think of *Zong!* in this context, even as I did earlier with the labels of post-modernism and language poetry. I strongly resist categorizing what I do as experimental, although the etymological traces in the word that link with acts of magic and sorcery are apt descriptors of the many tasks of poets. It is the connotation of testing, seeking evidential, empirical, or scientific proof that troubles me. I resist because we now live, have been living, will be living with the disastrous and cataclysmic effects of an experiment gone wrong—an ongoing experiment on a scale never seen before and which includes the almost total uprooting of the world's peoples and cultures by empire, colonialism, and capitalist depredations. England's "experiment in colonization"[61] continues to reverberate, as do the similar (un)successful experiments by other colonial powers. Troubling me further still is the implicit and explicit position of superiority of the ones who experiment; whether it be animal, vegetal, mineral, human—all aspects of life have been caught in the grand experiment that is modernity, the engine that grinds everything down to its lowest common denominator. I hasten to add that there is nothing within or about experimental poetry that approximates this commitment to mayhem—quite the contrary, in fact. However, in light of the project that claimed me—the struggle with a language that is my mother tongue but which refused to nurture and for whom I was but an experiment in nothing—to use that very word to describe what I do is anathema to me. As in the case of *She Tries*, even in naming, I resist, echoing or mirroring the formal properties of the disaster that the word experiment connotes for me.

None of this should be taken to mean that I object to how others categorize my work, nor should my arguments be interpreted as a critique of fellow poets, way-seekers like myself, who see themselves as experimental in the best sense of being innovative, or as introducing new ways of seeing and being in and with poetry. All approaches are necessary for our survival and this wounded world needs us all. Instead, I follow—"bloodspoored/the trail follows/me/following her/north/as far as not-known/I trace it."[62] I find myself at the (k)not-known that is poetry and sense that perhaps in and of itself poetry is always and already the ur-experiment, without the need for the "on," or the goal of establishing evidence or proof. Akin, perhaps, to the discipline of physics that uses mathematical formulae, the way we use words, rather than matter as their focus of query; or, perhaps even more assuring and contradictorily challenging, akin to the experiment that is the universe which simultaneously demonstrates and proposes the questions. That place of not (k)nowing, of the unfinished and the incomplete longing for . . .; the place where Then and Now collapse, late but always on time.

It is counterintuitive, if not contradictory, to suggest a rejection of the term experimental for my own work and yet intimate that it is poetry that is the experiment. I live with the contradiction—"english is my mother tongue . . . is my father tongue"—and await further clarity, if it ever arrives. Suffice it to say that in being the ur-experiment, poetry already and always is and we do not make poetry so much as poetry makes, unmakes, and remakes us—continually. And in making us it also marks us. Poetry is also where the known within the unknown resides, waiting to be re/cognized, as in to know and be known again and again. And again. The task or activity of discovering, uncovering, revealing the un(k)now(n)ing within the (k)now(n) is what we poets engage in and attempt—decoding the experiment that is poetry and, I'm tempted to say, life. It would be redundant of me, then, tautological even, to describe my strategies as a poet as experimental.

What the composition of *Zong!* taught me was how to let go of the ego; it continues to teach that—it is never easy or ever entirely successful. It continues to teach me how to absolve myself of authorship enough to recognize the existence of a deep-coded poetics that allows us to un/read and un/tell the world, as we must, if we are to survive. What I describe as the poetics of High Science, then, is perhaps a way to map and un/map the "ur-experiment," or the great question that is poetry, which is but the collision in time and space of time and space. It exceeds *logos*—the wor(l)d—and meaning even.

***

Several millennia later, late but on time, Then and Now collide through *Zong!* in the ancient oral art form *oríkì*, or praise song, as a result of which I now understand that the field within which we create extends across generations. How else to explain descriptions of this millennia-old art form that uncannily and accurately describe *Zong!?* "Porous and disjunctive"; a "dazzling juxtaposition of fragments"; "text(s) made of gaps"; a "jumble of fragments . . . of the past"; "the art of how to handle gaps." These are all descriptions of *oríkì*, an oral art form of the Yoruba which "are not concerned to present history so much as to simultaneously usher the past into the present and vice versa," and *oríkì* utterance achieves "meaning only in and through the concrete contexts of real, social existence."[63] I have not yet found more precise descriptions of what *Zong!* attempts in its formal strategies than these. Essentially poetic chants, *oríkì* are performed in as many different contexts as exist in a community—birth, death, marriage, and the honoring of divinities, politicians, and chiefs. *Oríkì* are chanted for animate and inanimate objects as well as for nature. I will not be presumptuous or disrespectful of a practice I do not know and say that performances of *Zong!*, whether solo or in a community of voices, function as contemporary Afrosporic expressions of *oríkì*, or transatlantic *oríkì* for the dead. *Oríkì* do, however, "make possible the crossing from the world of the dead to the world of the living, making the past present again."[64] And *Zong!*, by enmeshing itself in yet another manifestation of a poetics of relation, that links to an ancient art form, its people and practitioners—the Then, if you will—as well as to Afrosporic descendants who crossed the ga(s)p of water and time to enter the Now, accomplishes something similar. And through its insurgent potential, formal, architectural, and spiritual properties, the text attempts to repair the impossible, which is simultaneously not possible but entirely and urgently necessary.

Both the living and the dead "are interested in their Future,"[65] writes Lamming, describing the ceremony of Souls, a voudon ritual he witnessed many years ago in Port-au-Prince. This is what I believe *Zong!* facilitates—an understanding of how our own futures are linked to those (de)named Africans—"negro man," "negro woman"—on board the *Zong*, both the drowned and the survivors. None of this disputes or erases the Western literary genealogical roots of *Zong!*, but the existence across time of *oríkì*'s formal properties within *Zong!* collapses Then and Now—we may be late but still on time. And might I, perhaps, call this another manifesting of the poetics of High Science?

Some of these lessons have come at great expense of time and emotional energy, primarily witnessing and resisting the impulse on the part of those who desire to treat *Zong!* as fungible.[66] Alongside this approach, or perhaps very much a part of it, is the desire to turn the work into a metaphor or simile. These essentially extractive approaches are all of a piece with a transactional economic system that assigns value, in particular monetary value, to everything. "What they find hard to accept and therefore understand and integrate—much as they are ineluctably drawn to the text—is that there is something—magisterial perhaps (odd echo with magistrate), something serene, something that has to do with majesty at work in the text even as it deals with the profane, the obscenity and the murderousness of European attitudes to Black and African people."[67] Very little escapes the grasp of this system, including intellectual, artistic, and creative practices, some of our most significant meaning-making activities, which returns me to the central question that drove me as I untold the story that couldn't be told, yet had to be told: the story of the deliberate murder by drowning of some 150 enslaved Africans in order to collect insurance monies—the story of *Zong! As told to the author by Setaey Adamu Boateng*. How to make meaning—any meaning—of an act that while heinous and barbaric was also normal, ordinary and typical of its time? How would I—could I—make this event mean anything? And, therefore, perhaps, make it matter? What did happen on board the *Zong*? That was the question I asked in *Notanda* more than fifteen years ago as I embarked on the task of making memory matter—in all senses of the word. Fifteen years ago I suggested that all we could be sure of was that language had happened on board the *Zong*, and given that language is how we make meaning, and making meaning is central to our existence as beings who are human, who also live in language, perhaps these fifteen years later, language must still suffice as an answer. Celan's observation is apt here: "Only one thing remained reachable, close and secure amid all losses: language."[68] Fifteen years later, I still don't know what happened beyond language, but I embrace more fully the not-(k)nowing, the experiment that is poetry.

It is through language, in the meta sense that includes the visual, the sonic, and the auditory, that we attempt and tempt meaning, even when it appears as absence, silence—resisting our attempts to make meaning mean. When we gather to read the text, in a group large or small, or even in my solo readings, through the embodied breath that the form and text allow, which, perhaps more importantly, has the potential to repair and restore that which cannot be restored or repaired, we—i n i—make meaning matter literally, even as it continues to elude and resist us.

"There is nothing but meaning: our search for it, our flight from it, our struggle with it and, eventually, our embrace of it." In response to my writing this to a colleague, they reply that "that struggle is the embrace."[69] While the meaning of the *Zong* massacre and its memory made manifest in *Zong!* continue to elude me; when in performance I move aside to allow the possibility and potentiality in the space, in the gap that is the ga(s)p, to enter; when I allow the text to perform me, without the shame bestowed by history; when I embrace the un-telling of that which cannot, yet must be told; when I acknowledge that it, the text, cannot make meaning or even mean, at such times meaning becomes irrelevant, excess even.

With the exception of the structural organization of *Zong!*, nothing of what I have said about these texts should be taken as prescriptive. This exploration has simply been an attempt on my part to understand a difficult journey through history and memory via a contaminated language—a "foreign tongue" in which "the poet lies."[70] Essential lies, though, the better to get to the truth of a story begun in time "somewhere in Africa," to quote the Traveller, and equally somewhere in Europe or the United Kingdom. Somewhere. Here. There. All of which brings me to the geography and location of creation, which is so seminal to how and what we create. I have made a case that the formal aesthetics at work in *She Tries Her Tongue, Looking for Livingstone,* and *Zong!* derive from the Afro-Caribbean and West African thought and praxis, as well as being a part of the modernist Western tradition and its subsequent developments. I locate myself in a geography of creation which stretches from the tiny island Tobago—a deeply beloved place that is also the place of my birth; the matrix from which I write always. This geography stretches across an ocean and a sea— the Atlantic and the Caribbean—and connects a couple of continents to recreate yet another triangle, this time a triangle of influence, resistance, and creation. While not overtly about the Caribbean, these three texts, *She Tries Her Tongue, Looking for Livingstone*, and *Zong!*, are rooted deeply in that culture, history, and geography. Defying time and the depredations of history, however, something appears to have persisted from that time of "not-known": "when I return/woad-skinned with grief/welcome me gently/I carry tiny thorns of Africa . . ."[71]

Counterintuitively, however, these works could only have been written in Canada, for had I remained in the Caribbean, I would not have had the perspective that distance from the source demands and affords, as Lamming so brilliantly explores in *Pleasures*. Had I instead emigrated to the United Kingdom—the Mother Country as it was for so many—the weight and power of that tradition would have intimidated and crushed my imagination, despite the existence of a long history of writing from the outlying empire and its colonies. So too in the United States where the depth and complexity of the African American literary tradition going back to Phillis Wheatley would have demanded that I subsume my interests in my own very specific colonial experience to what was and still is most pressing there for African Americans—getting out from under the raw, unmitigated power of the most powerful country in the world—empire redux. It is, however, important to note that in ways too numerous to explore here, their struggle is also ours. It was Canada, settler nation that it is, that offered a certain space—akin perhaps to the breath-space of *Zong!*—within which I could create these works, albeit on the margins, but margins which I would convert into a metaphorical frontier.

Despite its negative connotations within the colonial project, the idea of being on the frontier proved more useful than thinking of myself as being on the margins. It meant that everything behind me was the hinterland on which I could turn my back. On the frontier you made your own rules, which was helpful in trying to understand what I was rejecting and what I wanted to retain. For instance, the importance and use of the demotic, or nation language, was vital to me as a writer, but I sensed that it would not be recognized, let alone be welcomed in mainstream poetry circles. The absence of a critical presence of Black and African Canadian writers at that time also contributed to the feeling of profound isolation and of being up against an invisible wall of silence created by a colonial, English-derived culture, replete with its own cultural insecurities and determinedly committed to its own sense of cultural and racial superiority. The choice appeared stark—indeed, there was no choice and in retrospect

I am stunned by how tenuous my expectation for myself was in the face of such massive indifference: "I think I might have something to say." A gossamer-thin thread of belief that someone somewhere just might be interested in that "something." In owing their existence to this place and space called Canada, these three works, *She Tries Her Tongue*, *Looking for Livingstone*, and *Zong!*, that grew from the kernel of the "something" I had to say, can also be seen as Canadian. In one of the most startling ironies of my writing life, however, it would be the United States that would later save me as a poet and writer. At a time when I had become disappeared as a poet in Canada because of my activism against the culturally and racially biased practices of arts councils and other cultural institutions, the engagement with my work by fellow poets and scholars in the US helped me to trust myself and my instincts and to believe in the work I was doing. For this act of generous receptivity, I remain enduringly grateful.

The historical underpinnings of the entity—the forensic landscape we now call Canada—which afforded me a breathing space, are rooted in the extinguishment of breath and life for the Indigenous of this land, Turtle Island. In the long durée and seemingly unending cycles of global exploitation precipitated by the age of empire and colonialism, the experiences of the Indigenous and of Black and African-descended people in this new but so-very-old world are intricately linked, indeed constitute the same experiment against life itself.[72]

Despite being in Canada for more than half a century, I still feel a sense of destabilization, both here and in my country of birth. A destabilization begun centuries ago by imperial and colonial regimes and writ large today as the world heats and large groups of migrants are on the move, as the brutal legacies of colonialism heave and turn wretchedly.

> There is a sense in which I understand the entire book to be destabilized and that the text is actually working to stabilize or "right" itself. I am also thinking that it's trying to right something destabilized in time and history . . . One could argue that the text enacts a sort of verbal proprioception in that by constantly adjusting itself to the spaces above, below and around it, it is engaged in a continuous and ongoing act of adjusting itself in relation to the other parts of the text. As well as to history, lower and upper case; to time and to Silence. The text itself is constantly shifting.[73]

As are we. Perhaps, even as it eludes and escapes the net of meaning, *Zong!* accomplishes what might be seen as a temporary and momentary proprioceptive stabilization in a world that remains profoundly destabilized. It works to anchor, for the eternity of a moment, all that is awry and out of joint. Perhaps, also, in a world so burdened with meaning, and the impulse always to make meaning and all that flows from that effort, the opportunity to enter the gap within the ga(s)p, where space, time, sound, and sometimes movement collide to create intervals, however momentary, however temporary, that resist meaning and the urge to make meaning, perhaps that opportunity becomes a gift whose exorbitance itself resists meaning. Always. Arriving late on time . . . in time . . . "the *oba* sobs" . . .

in on &
over
itself
the text   redoubles
returns to source
forever
always
on
time
in
time
late
in time   like starlight
always[74]

And for that i n i must always be. And Am. Grateful.

m. nourbeSe philip
August 2023

Coda or the B-Archive of *Zong!*

Using a metaphor culled from an older musical tradition of records, I contend that if *Gregson v. Gilbert* is the A-side of the legal archive, then *Zong!* represents the B-side of that archive. The side that is often dismissed and perceived as not fitting the norm or the expected—I would add even perhaps the submerged side. On Saturday, March 23, 2024, *Zong!* entered the Afrosonic[75] realm where that archive lives and has always lived. On that day a group of musicians[76] and myself, using techno, electronic sounds, and beats along with guitar, bass, drum, percussion, and vocals, opened the entire text of the book to performance, including—astonishingly so—the accompanying essays, Glossary, Manifest, and case report. I have often performed *Zong!* within the context of acoustic music; this was, however, the first time that electronic sound had been added, and it appeared as if the text had been waiting for this sound, its sound—the glorious and challenging sound of the Afrosonic B-archive.

NOTES

1. m. nourbeSe philip, *Zong! As told to the author by Setaey Adamu Boateng* (Wesleyan University Press, Middleton, CT, 2008).

2. Ifá is the name of the spiritual practice of the Yoruba people of West Africa, found predominantly in Nigeria but also in neighbouring countries. A central part of the practice is divination, which involves casting cowries or palm nuts that are then read and linked to the appropriate verse or *odu*. These verses are a combination of proverbs, stories, and poetry that describe, often cryptically, human and animal behaviour that are interpreted by the divining priest, the *babalao*.

3. Zen Buddhist expression that presents as a riddle or a story intended to stimulate reflection.

4. The genesis for these readings was a conversation I had in 2012 with the scholar Colleen Asper, during which she shared with me that Fred Moten had recently instructed his class to read *Zong!* simultaneously and collectively. The moment was epiphanic—as soon as I heard her say that, I knew that was how *Zong!* had to be read: it had to be choric. Every year since 2012, on or about November 29, the date the massacre began on board the *Zong*, I have organized an annual, durational public reading of *Zong!* where all who attend are invited to participate in reading the entire text over several hours. Music and dance are often an integral part of the event.

5. m. nourbeSe philip, *She Tries Her Tongue; Her Silence Softly Breaks* (Wesleyan University Press, Middleton, CT, 2015).

6. *Ibid.*, p. 10.

7. The unusual orthography of the word "S/silence" arises from the tension between the silencing that results from colonial practices of silence and silencing and another type of Silence generated from within and that runs the gamut from resistance in the face of illegitimate power to a necessary Silence required for listening, for instance, or even to the Silence generated by awe in the face of nature—the ocean, the forest, the desert, the night sky.

8. m. nourbeSe philip, *Looking for Livingstone: An Odyssey of Silence* (The Centre for Expanded Poetics and Anteism, Montreal, 2018).

9. See note 5 above, p. 30.

10. T. S. Eliot repurposed the idea of the objective correlative developed by American painter and poet Washington Allston for use in literature and literary analysis.

11. See note 5 above, p. 32.

12. *Ibid.*, p. 82.

13. *Ibid.*, p. 84.

14. *Ibid.*, p. 47.

15. After the Second World War, the poet Paul Celan expressed the view that German had been sullied by hate speech and propaganda. He believed that the language had to be cleansed to make it "safe" again for poetry. It has intrigued me that colonial languages, like English, for instance, have never been seen to be contaminated or sullied, or in need of cleansing.

16. July 6, 2015, email written in Nigeria to a colleague. Although this was written about a visit to Bordeaux and my reluctance to even attempt to speak French, which I studied for seven years and still read fluently, it is also about my mother tongue English.

17. See note 5 above, p. 82.

18. *Ibid.*, p. 32.

19. See note 8 above, p. 17.

20. *Ibid.*, p. 77.

21. See note 5 above, p. 37. Esu and Legba are two gods in the *Ifá* pantheon of the Yoruba people of West Africa.

22. See note 27 of *Notanda*.

23. *Zong!*, p. 43.

24. *Ibid.*, p. 20.

25. Conversation with the scholar Faizal Deen, December 2021.

26. What excites me profoundly as a poet is confirmation of a long-held belief about the connections and links between poetry and geometry.

27. I use the prefix "diss" to suggest not only an absence of fluency but as a critique of fluency.

28. "Exaqua" first used in *Notanda*, p. 201.

29. Trinbagonian vernacular way of saying, "what it did to us and what we're doing to it in response."

30. Documentary filmmaker Alexandra Gelis through her installation "Seeds" introduced me to this practice of the people of Palenque, Colombia. The *lumbalu*, which Gelis refers to as a tunnel of sound, bears significant similarities to the nine-night funerary rituals of the Afro-Caribbean.

31. See note 1 above, p. 63.

32. Trinbagonian vernacular expression for that time just before day becomes morning, usually to the sound of crowing cocks.

33. The poet Charles Bernstein has been credited with describing poets as being responsible for the research and development component of language. I would like to add to that description the aspect of quality control.

34. Email from m. nourbeSe philip to Benway Series, dated June 15, 2021. In the Spring of 2021, Benway Series, Italy, over my strenuous objections, published a mistranslation of *Zong!*, which failed to observe the organizational principle of the text. The email explained in detail what was wrong with the mistranslation and asked that they not publish it. Please see: "Considering the Dystranslation of *Zong!*" Interview with Barbara Ofosu-Somuah (*Violent Phenomena*, edited by Kavita Bhanot and Jeremy Tiang. Tilted Axis Press, 2022, pp. 287-304).

35. See note 5 above, p. 56.

36. George Lamming, *The Pleasures of Exile* (Ann Arbor, University of Michigan Press, 2004), pp. 9-13.

37. This reference is an homage to Fred Moten's seminal work of the same name, *In the Break*.

38. In the aftermath of a recent reading, I shared this idea with the audience and was later approached by a member of the audience who drew my attention to the "Jewish concept of reading the white behind the black letters in a Torah scroll." Email to m. nourbeSe philip, dated June 5, 2023.

39. See note 5 above, p. 58.

40. *Ibid.*, p. 64.

41. African American spiritual, "Swing Low, Sweet Chariot."

42. Bob Marley, "Redemption Song" (Uprising, Island/Tuff Gong, 1980).

43. David Rudder, "Haiti I'm Sorry" (Haiti, Sire, Lypsoland, London, 1988).

44. Black Stalin, "Bun Dem," 1987.

45. The members of The Zong! Quartet were myself, Brenda Joy Lem, Mike Leigh, and Colin Anthony.

46. "Considering the Dystranslation of *Zong!*" Interview with Barbara Ofosu-Somuah (*Violent Phenomena*, edited by Kavita Bhanot and Jeremy Tiang. Tilted Axis Press, 2022, pp. 287-304).

47. Doption is a practice of rhythmic breathing during worship by followers of the Spiritual Baptist faith, which is practiced in Trinidad and Tobago and other Caribbean countries.

48. Édouard Glissant, *Poetics of Relation* (Ann Arbor, University of Michigan Press, 1997).

49. Conversation with Evie Shockley, January 2023. Conjure is an African-rooted form of spirituality, which was transported to the "New World" along with its practitioners, enslaved Africans. It is also known as hoodoo or root work, the latter word referring to the use of herbs and roots. It was widely practiced through the southern states, and particularly in New Orleans.

50. In a startling lexical reversal in Trinidad and Tobago, practitioners of the creolized West African-based spiritual and healing practice obeah, in the face of its dismissal and criminalization as superstition and magic within the Western paradigm of colonial societies, have co-opted the word "science" into the expression High Science to mean an elevated level of this tradition.

51. Obeah is the creolized spiritual practice rooted in West African traditions and which was made illegal by colonial law.

52. "i n i" is an expression used in the Rastafarian community to express the idea that even as you refer to yourself, you acknowledge that each individual is a part of something larger, whether it be community or the Creator or both.

53. June 11, 2021, email to Benway Publishers criticizing their mistranslation of *Zong!*

54. *Maafa* is a Swahili word meaning a terrible and awful experience, which some use to refer to the transatlantic trade in Africans as well as slavery.

55. June 14, 2021, email to colleague regarding Benway Series mistranslation of *Zong!*

56. Spiritual or Shouter Baptists are a sect of Christianity that were also outlawed under colonialism because their forms of worship contained too many Africanisms.

57. *Okyeame* is an Ashanti word which roughly translates to Linguist, an official position within royal culture, in which the office holder becomes a member of the King's retinue whose role is to facilitate communication between the Ancestors, the King, and the people. The *Okyeame*'s role also includes judicial and political duties.

58. See note 5 above, p. 56.

59. See note 1 above, p. 204.

60. See note 34 above.

61. See note 36 above.

62. See note 5 above.

63. Karin Barber, *I Could Speak Until Tomorrow: Oriki, Women and the Past in a Yoruba Town* (Edinburgh, Edinburgh University Press, 1991).

64. *Ibid.*

65. See note 36 above.

66. About this Katherine McKittrick writes: "The affectual-political aesthetics, the research, the writing, the creative labour, the physiological-psychic energy expended to make *Zong!* what it is, are absorbed by the assumptive logic of the requestions (the assumptive logics are importantly quotidian). The absorption reveals that both the poet and the poetry cycle are, according to some at

least, fungible." (*The Funambulist,* July-August 2022, "Agony, Thoughtfully, Carefully")

67. See note 34 above.

68. Ruth Franklin, "How Paul Celan Reconceived Language for a Post-Holocaust World" (*New Yorker,* November 16, 2020).

69. Email exchange with Charles Bernstein dated November 14, 2020.

70. See note 68 above.

71. Marlene Philip, *Thorns* (Toronto, Williams Wallace, 1980).

72. In *The Need for Roots,* Simone Weil argues that the European, after uprooting himself of his own culture and traditions, set about to uproot the rest of the world. It's important to be aware of the intersecting aspects of empire—profits from the Caribbean gained through exploitation of enslaved Africans were used to enrich the British crown and its ruling classes. Those profits were also used to support their exploitative expansion into and colonization of the white-ruled Dominions such as Canada and Australia.

73. Email from m. nourbeSe philip to Julie Joosten dated November, 2019.

74. In May 2023, I participated in a discussion at UC Irvine in which I introduced the idea of being late but on time. A student in the PhD program in Humanities would later make reference to the fact that starlight was the embodiment of this idea of being late but on time.

75. Dr. Mark V. Campbell, *Afrosonic Life* (New York, Bloomsbury, 2022).

76. Mike Lynn, upright bass; Mark Campbell, turntable; Y Josephine, cajón; Brenda Joy Lem, percussion and vocals; Amai Kuda, vocals; Kuda Mutamba, guitar. The performance was held at It's Ok Studios, Toronto. Clips can be seen on m. nourbeSe philip's YouTube channel.

Stars, Actually

... the drain from Africa ran into the millions.
C. L. R. James, *The Black Jacobins*

In her discussion of the diagram of the slave ship *Brookes*, Simone Browne uncovers some of the layered narratives that complemented the forced transportation of black people across the Middle Passage. Noting how the image delineates the perimeters that enclosed and injured those it carried, she also offers a series of insights that are tethered to the diagram, but cannot be fully expressed by it. What cannot be expressed, what the diagram doesn't enunciate, are moments of intimacy, violence, and quiet observation. What cannot be expressed, what surrounds and moves through the image, are soundscapes of "refusal, freedom, and rebellion."[1] Many of us know the *Brookes* image well, we are familiar with this portrayal of objecthood, we remember looking at a ship just like this in 2005, we know and teach the history of these ships (*I saw one yesterday*). I read of the ship compulsively.[2] We have studied these ships alongside George Lamming and Paul Gilroy and Kara Walker. The *Brookes* diagram is not simply a ship but a program for the maximization of profits by extracting humanity from black people. The illustration unfolds: the objective is tied to the conceptual intent and requires collective approval; harm is actualized. It situates the living memory of slavery in relation to geographies of transport, ecologies of ocean and water, and the physicality of the ship itself (wood and other organic and non-organic materials).[3] Like *Brookes*, like other vessels, the slave ship *Zong* is an architecture of ephemeral inexpression and ecological re-memory.[4] (*I cannot tell you about the ship I imagined yesterday, it was on the ocean, it was bursting with terribleness.*)

    m. nourbeSe philip's *Zong!* is a composition of ephemeral inexpression and ecological re-memory that is saturated with black livingness and this black livingness is trace

---

1. Simone Browne, *Dark Matters: On the Surveillance of Blackness* (Duke University Press, 2015).

2. Édouard Glissant, *Poetics of Relation*, trans. Betsy Wing (1990; rpt.: University of Michigan Press, 1997).

3. I borrow "living memory" from Paul Gilroy, *The Black Atlantic: Modernity and Double Consciousness* (Harvard University Press, 1993) pp. 186-223.

4. Toni Morrison, *Beloved* (Plume, 1987).

(*what happened on that ship, what happened after the massacre, what happened after it landed, I barely recall*). Her rendering of black loss is stretched between regimes of racism and spectral poetics. In *Zong!* the words are scattered and perfectly placed. The words are not read with ease. The words are collected and unravel as stories of frenzy and sunken songs and weeks and months and cold. I often recall, daily in fact, where she writes of stars:

> do the stars   shine   if only
>   murder made us   you were by my side

The final pages of *Zong!* include a Glossary and a Manifest. The former is columns of words with translations (Arabic, Dutch, Fon, French, Hebrew, Portuguese, Shona, Yoruba, and more) towards English. The Glossary—words and phrases heard aboard the *Zong*—offers an unsettling clarity. Loss is linguistically deciphered and translated (*aide moi*: help; *belo*: beautiful; *ilé wa*: our house). This is what was heard. The Manifest lists the ship's contents (crew, body parts, animals, African groups and languages, women who wait, nature, food and drink). The function of a manifest is to prove and document and identify the ship's contents; sky, sea, mist, and ocean are also listed in the Manifest.

At the end of *Zong!* the legal summary of *Gregson v. Gilbert*, the case that followed the massacre, is presented. It lays bare the intensity of the story, the actualization of the plan, the fulfillment of misery: due to navigational errors that resulted in extended time at sea, due to navigational errors that resulted in financial loss, hundreds of Africans aboard the ship were tossed into the sea. The murder recuperated the financial loss; financial loss was regained through racial terror.

At the end of *Zong!*, in *Notanda*, philip maps her methodology. She writes of her decision (summons) to read across the legal archive. She takes that archive and lacerates it, gives it to us anew—as a poetry cycle, as the voices of the lost, as the incomprehensibility of violence. Agony.

Notanda, *Gregson v. Gilbert*, the Glossary, and the Manifest close *Zong!* Yet this network of ideas and ecologies and names and items and expressions and legal proceedings wander beneath the main text, forwardly, to shape the poetic iteration, "Os." And we soon learn that *Zong!*, in fact, has no beginning and that the ending—the closing network of ideas—is provisional. The temporality of *Zong!* is intractable; this is why, perhaps, the stars are forever, and why the story in front of us is an ineffable and heartbreaking and incalculable gift.

Katherine McKittrick

Introduction

Sonic compositions emerge from the hold of the ship. Groans and cries, unheeded laments, moans, melancholy noise comprise the earliest fragments of testimony and slave narrative. Among the utterances tumbling across the diagrammatic pages of *Zong!* are the ambient sounds of the hold. It is possible to discern the muffled voice of the young Ottobah, the heartbeat of an African girl-child not yet erased by the name Phillis and too terrified to scream, Kussola's weeping, a meagre child mourning the mother lost to the watery grave, a man pleading for death. Word clusters and blossoms of phonemes clot the pages of *Zong!*, dense with beauty and death, thick with want, with prayers and crying voices, with thirst and frenzy, with the sobs of the *oba*, with the cold reason of law, with the calculus of insurance, with the ledger's columns of loss and gain, with the ruthless opining and ironclad judgments of the British ruling elite, with the murderous *ratio* of the law.

The violence and brutality of the transatlantic slave trade unfold in and as the drama of language. The way of death is conjured in recurring phrases extracted from the limited legal template of *Gregson v. Gilbert*, and its impossibly inadequate description of what happened on board the *Zong*, its failed recounting of this particular event of loss, the jettisoning of 150 captives cast overboard into the Atlantic. This violence saturates language; language saturates violence. Words like *slave, cargo, reason*, and *truth* provide the foundation of a modern world built on accumulation, the negated being of Africans, controlled depletion, and black death. This order of things is sedimented in casual and neutral turns of phrases, in the formula: subject verb predicate, in the verb and its object, in grammar and syntax. To disassemble the word is to disassemble the ordered world. Every volume written by m. nourbeSe philip has been nurtured by this insight.

How then does *Zong!* make good the promise of undoing the compelled utterance, breaking the hold of *the discourse on language*? How is philip able to fashion poems from the "modest report" of a legal case? How might the template of a two-page judicial opinion, which consigns black life to the category of commodity, deems it fungible and disposable, and relegates the captive to death, provide a word store capable of sustaining and reanimating black life? Or yield stories housed in no one's archive? Or condense the history of modernity and reason, and illuminate the stolen life and land that is its bedrock in 200 pages? *Zong!* achieves the seemingly impossible, using the law to generate story, and translating the generic loss of property into a memorial text that glimpses life on the brink of disappearance.

m. nourbeSe philip utilizes the incantatory power of the fragment, and *surrenders her abrasive words to us*, not to make a whole, but to compose a beautiful shattered work. The visual array of letters on the page, the dense thickets of sounds and opaque utterance, the broken words and refused syntax, disorients and arrests us in our tracks. *Zong!* holds and suspends us in the Atlantic, immersed in *the residence time of the wake*. The long poem and its movement challenge us to read the story that is impossible to tell, striving to tell by not telling. By stumbling, by withholding, by the pure force of sound, guttural, sibilant, diphthong, by jargon and nonsense, by strings of letters adrift from proper words, by *phonic substance* not tethered to signification, by orthographies of the unspeakable, by the polyvocality of the text, by *the polyglotta Africana* of the ship's hold, by the palimpsest of layered phrases and names and shards of experience that will never cohere into narrative, the fragments of black life and death that will never be folded into a plot or bildung. *Zong!* mutilates language and murders the imposed tongue. It revels in the tumult of words and perpetrates a joyous destruction. The daughter's *malevolent tongue*, now tried, offers not redress, but a reckoning that yields song, a dirge and celebration of black life and survivance. The words crosscutting the page are like a ladder allowing us to climb on board, like a wormhole to three months of want and atrocity in 1781, like a lifeline keeping us afloat in the vast sea of death. The rush of words: the truth of words fail and fall, the truth of words falls overboard, *sow[ing]/the seas/with she negroes* and black corpses, truth *rimed with sin/her sex/open all night rain*. All night rain. We fall with her and with them, overwhelmed by the surfeit of words, the many voices reverberating on these pages.

A reading of *Zong!* that attempts to restore meaning, confer legibility, suture fragments is doomed to fail and is beside the point. As philip writes: "the poem escapes the net of complete understanding."

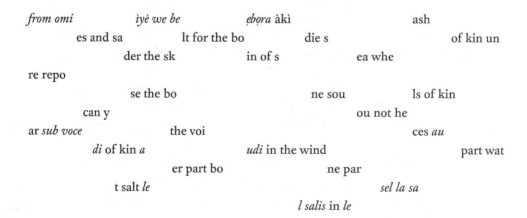

An example, a glimmer of meaning: *ashes and salt for the bodies of kin under the skin of sea where repose the bone souls of kin. can you not hear sub voce, can you not hear the voices, audi of kin, audi in the wind, part water, part bone, part salt.* An attempt to sort and order the language, to make the opaque legible, to create a line from a helix of words, to confer meaning where there is none betrays the very thing that *Zong!* demands of us, that we sit with the limits of what we can know, accept the unspeakable character of what has transpired, acknowledge what can't be recovered, surrender to it, be dispossessed by the enormity of absence. *Words need a lot of space to breathe.* To bridge fragments into a continuous line, to suture and repair broken words, arrange the disorder, or lessen the tumult risks misreading. The poem refuses easy fixes or grids of intelligibility. *Zong!* demands everything of the reader and offers no guarantees that you won't get lost along the journey. Get stuck, find yourself at conceptual impasse which requires you to abandon everything you think you know, and figure out again how to do something as basic as read.

The rupture cannot be bridged or repaired, it simply must be entered, one must endure the absence of signposts, surrender to the cacophony of voices, live with the bones in water, endure the violence of the cargo being made into whore and taken, falling overboard, pulled along in the wake of the ship entering the cunt of the sea:

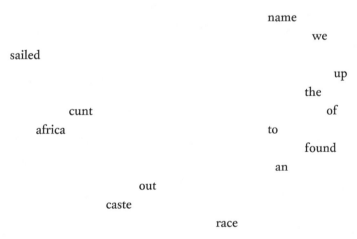

How do we read such a work? The poem offers little instruction, although the para-textual materials, the Glossary, the Manifest, the Notanda, the end notes, and the legal document help us navigate the oceanic. *A sufficient quantity of water did not remain on board, for want of water for sustenance, threw themselves into the sea and were drowned, consequence of which the negroes were thrown overboard, there appeared in evidence no sufficient necessity, in throwing the negroes overboard, the rains came on, which furnished water for eleven days, notwithstanding which more of the negroes were thrown overboard.* These murderous words appear in seemingly interminable combination, the law of property provides the storehouse; yet all the anagrammatical variations and possible combinations are still not adequate to tell the story, or elude the violence of reason. Tautology as episteme: *was the cause was the remedy was the record was the argument . . . negroes was the cause.* (*Zong!* #26)

clear the law

of

order

cause

delay

of question

&

opinion

of the etc of negroes

The movement is from bone to flesh: *os, sal, ventus, ratio, ferrum, ebora*. The multiple pathways of the poem thwart any straightforward approach. The line doesn't break, the page does, language is rent, words are shattered, grammar as a mechanism of force is defeated, no commas or periods, just negative space that suggests less a place to pause than it conveys the experience of being adrift, of falling, of breathing, of drowning, of perduring and waiting with no palliative of rescue or refuge. We are forced to suffer not knowing, we follow the word trails ignorant of where they will take us, we read without assurances about the certainty of meaning and doubting how to read, so we scan the page gathering phrases and terms and unfamiliar expressions, even as we desire to make sense of things, even as we are unable to deny that reason is inseparable from the murders recounted, from the lives overboard. Should the eye move across the page or down a column? Does one make sense of the broken line or repair and reassemble the shattered word? How does one read the multiple and simultaneous utterances of the page? The work is a refusal of the imposed language, line and metre, transparency. The only certainty is the constancy and necessity of experiment in the wake of loss. The visual arrangement of letters on the page and the broken words, the negative space and nonconventional orthography, the fragmented and discontinuous presentation of story, the legal terms, the Latin phrases, the strains of Shona and Yoruba, the competing columns signal the multitude of voices and the impossibility of any settled meaning.

The form of *Zong!* is unanticipated even by its presumed author. In the course of its writing, philip yielded to the work, as she observes, letting the poem write itself. Across the body of the poem, a series of concerns about the violence of language and the law, silence standing in for words and interrupting, creating caesuras and absences in the stories of the *Zong*. The unsaid, the unspeakable, shapes the poem, breaks the fragments into a proliferation of stories about slaves overboard, captive Africans dying for want of water, first mates loving and lying and whoring and writing, dearest dido, myth and daughter, sired onboard a slaver, a captain's suicide. The silence embedded in each word is made apparent in the breaking up of words, where the slippage and rush of words or the cut of the backslash/sunders and propagates, as it highlights the instability of meaning and makes multiple readings possible. The breaking of words insinuates the bodies broken and the rupture of the Middle Passage. Words are reduced to sounds, consonants and gutturals unmoored from meaning, registering only the force and frequency of sonic utterance, the commands impossible to understand even when translated: jump.

Zong! is a phonography of the hold. It is an open text, a chant shout from the abyss. The babel of voices, the dissonant vocality of strange tongues, the rasp and murmur of breath, the echo and roar of the sea. This song of the fragment, a song of destruction and survival, negation and death, a song of the afterlife, is a lament for the millions gone and for what lives on. *Zong!* is desecration and elegy. It is the song of an untold story, a story not to be passed on, a contrapuntal fugue in which we listen for the dead.

Saidiya Hartman

Acknowledgments

My deepest gratitude to all those who have, over the years, attended and participated in the annual durational readings of *Zong! As told to the author by Setaey Adamu Boateng*. Thank you for remembering with me those who were discarded as so much flotsam and jetsam; most importantly thank you for making the annual journey in and through time that always ends in joy. Thank you for taking *Zong!* off the page and reclaiming it in sound and music and dance.

A huge wave of gratitude and appreciation suffused with awe to the musicians and dancers, in particular, Colin, Kwabena, Y, Brenda, Mike, Amai, Sistah Lois, and Cheryl O, Vivine, and Natasha. A special thank you to Muna for bringing the sonic vibes.

To all the readers from around the world who summoned *Zong!* to the digital world by participating in the *Zong! Global* 2020 online reading, a joyous shout out of gratitude, as well as to those who were a part of the 2021 online event, *RevrrrbOrashuns*. More particularly, massive gratitude to those who in one way or another helped to bring both these events to the screen and world: Richard, Faizal, Diane, Zoe, Natasha, Katherine, Elena, the Black Studies Program, Queens University, and the Transnational Law and Justice Network, University of Windsor. As well, thanks to our tech support, Collective Broadcasting, without which neither of these events would have been possible.

A special thank you to Tonya and Julie for their help in bringing this edition of *Zong!* to completion, late but very much on time. Julie's contributions to the editing of the preface have been invaluable and are deeply appreciated.

For the late, late, late night conversations in which we stop the world and start it again, deep gratitude, love, and appreciation to Faizal, fellow member of the biphasic sleep tribe.

Many, many thanks to Katherine and Saidiya for honouring *Zong!* by lending their brilliance to this edition. Deep acknowledgment to Silver Press for being willing to walk the walk, difficult as it was.

To all my friends, here and elsewhere, young and old, poets, writers, artists, free thinkers, and dancers, your friendship has been an inestimable boon to me and you all, each in your own way, have helped me to survive the challenges that *Zong!*'s movement through life has brought and your friendship has become a part of that survival.

As always, to Paul, Bruce, Hardie, Amai, and Kuda—magnificent love. Being family in all its complicatedness is the sine qua non of all of the above.

And, to the island of Tobago on which I stand always—a humble bow of gratitude.

Ox

The sea was not a mask.

WALLACE STEVENS

Zong! #1

w   w   w   w   a   wa

               w   a   w   a   t

er   wa   s

        our   wa

te   r gg   g   g   go

     o   oo   goo   d

     waa   wa wa

w w waa

     ter   o   oh

on   o   ne   w one

        w o n   d d d

   ey   d   a

dey   a   ah   ay

  s   one   day s

     wa   wa

Masuz Zuwena Ogunsheye Ziyad Ogwambi Keturah

w w w w w   a

w wa   wa   t

er   wa   te

r   wat

er   wa   ter

of   w

ant

Aba Chimanga Naeema Oba Eshe

Zong! #2

                                        the throw in circumstance

                the weight in want

                                in sustenance

        for underwriters

                                the loss

        the order in destroy

                                the that fact

                                the it was

                                the were

negroes

                                the after rains

Zong! #3

        the some of negroes

              over

board

the rest in lives

              drowned

exist did not

              in themselves

preservation

              obliged

frenzy

thirst for forty others

              etc

Zong! #4

                              this is

          not was

                        or

                  should be

            this be

                        not

    should be

                        this

          should

                        not

            be

  is

Lipapwiche Aziza Chipo Dada Nomsa

Zong! #5

          of

water

rains &

dead

        the more

    of

        the more

    of

negroes

              of

        water

        &

        weeks

          (three less than)

      rains

Asabi Nomusa Oje Ibijoke Abiona

&

water

(three butts good)

of

sea and

perils

of water

(one day)

water —

day one ...

of months

of

weeks

of

days

of

sustenance

lying

dead

———————————————————

Mwita Muhammad Mulogo Becktemba Hadiya

of

days

of

sour water

enemies &

want

of

died

(seven out of seventeen)

of

good

(the more of)

of

(eighteen instead of six)

dead

of rains

(eleven days)

of

weeks

(thirty not three)

Odusanya Mxali Ogunba

                              of

                                                  water

                                                      day one . . .

for sustenance

                                                  water

                                                          day

one . . .

one day's

                                                  water

                                                          day

one . . .

sour

                                                  water

                                                          day

one . . .

three butts good

                        of voyage

                        (a month's)

of necessity

sufficient

and

last

the more

of

exist

want &

less than

of did not

&

the more of

of suffered

did not

exist

sustenance

water &

want

of

Ngolinda Amina Kiambu Ngunda Nobanzi

dead

the more of

of negroes

the more

of

instead

of

Zong! #6

question therefore

the age

eighteen weeks

and calm

but it is said . . .

— from the maps

and

contradicted

by the evidence . . .

question

therefore

the age

Zuka Tuwalole Urbi Femi Chuma

Zong! #7

first:

the when

the which

the who

the were

the throwing

overboard

the be

come apprehended

exist did not

Zong! #8

the good of overboard

justified a throwing

                    of property

                       fellow

creatures

         become

                  our portion

                       of

                  mortality

        provision

                 a bad market

negroes

                      want

        for dying

Abioye Gulai Sekelaga Dalili N'Nanna

Zong! #9

                                              slaves

                                    to the order in

          destroyed

                              the circumstance in

          fact

                                    the property in

          subject

                                      the subject in

          creature

                                          the loss in

          underwriter

                                    to the fellow in

          negro

                                      the sustenance

          in want

_____

                              the arrived

in vessel

                              the weight

in provisions

                              the suffered in

 die

                              the me in

become

Zong! #10

should have

        was reduced

          retarded

          rendered

               could

found

given

sailed

bring to

              occurred

throwing

              arose

to be

was

were

              passed

justify

              appeared

authorize

              made might

Oluseyi Fatoki Abifarin Soremekun Kwakou

Zong! #11

                    suppose the law

                            is

not

                        does

not

                      would

not

                         be

not

suppose the law not

                 — a crime

suppose the law a loss

suppose the law

suppose

Zong! #12

    it

        is said

        has been decided

        was justified

        appeared impossible

        is not necessary

        is another ground

        need not be proved

it

    was a throwing overboard

        it

        is a particular circumstance

        need not be proved

        is another ground

        is not necessary

        appeared impossible

Oni Sanura Mashama Sigolwide Shamfa

was justified

has been decided

is said

it

was

Zong! #13

the rest of

the more of

the half of

out of

fifty of

instead of

negroes

the necessity of

Zong! #14

the truth was

        the ship sailed

        the rains came

        the loss arose

                the truth is

the ship sailed

the rains came

the loss arose

                the negroes is

the truth was

Zong! #15

defend the dead

        weight of circumstance

ground

      to usual &

         etc

        where the ratio of just

in less than

       is necessary

          to murder

the subject in property

the save in underwriter

         where etc tunes justice

         and the *ratio* of murder

         is

         the usual in occurred

Akilah Falope Ouma Weke Jubade

the just in ration

the suffer in loss

defend the dead

the weight

in

circumstance

ached in necessary

the ration in just

age the act in the *ave* to justice

Micere Ndale Omowunmi Ramla Ajani

Zong! #16

should they have

found being

                sufficient

                a necessity

(portion that question)

should they have

                found the justify

for exist

                a rule for new

                the policy within the loss

(portion that question etc)

should they —

might they have

                found

Nompumelelo Okulaja Ekisola Abike Arike

the of and during & wherefore

the preserving

the insurance of water

the within loss

the terms of exist

a negro of wit

should they have found

water

&

being

sufficient

Zong! #17

there was

    the this

    the that

    the frenzy

        leaky seas &

          casks

          negroes of no belonging

on board

no rest

    came the rains

    came the negroes

    came the perils

    came the owners

        master and mariners

Adunni Akanni Akanbi Alade Alayande

                                                    the this

                                                    the that

                                                    the frenzy

came the insurance of water

water of good only

came water sufficient

that was truth

& seas of mortality

                                        question the now

                            the this

                            the that

                            the frenzy

not unwisely

Zong! #18

means

truth

means overboard

means

sufficient

means support

means

foul

means three butts

means

necessity

means provisions

means

perils

Toyin Sipho Adelabu Lisabi Fayemi Eki

<pre>
      means   evidence

                        means

mortality

      means   policy

                        means

voyage

      means   market

                        means

slaves

      means   more

                        means

dead

      means   want

water

      means   water
</pre>

Zong! #19

drowned the law

      their thirst &

      the evidence

      obliged the frenzy

in themselves

in the sea

      ground the justify

      in the necessity of

when

who &

which

there is no evidence

            in the against of winds

the consequence of currents

        or

            the apprehension of rains

the certain of value

        or

            the value in certain

against the rest in preservation

            the save in residue

negroes exist

            for the throwing

Zong! #20

this necessity of loss

this quantity of not

perils underwriters

insurers

of

the throw in circumstance

the instance in attempt

the attempt in voyage

the may in become

in

the between of day

a sea of negroes

drowned

live

in the thirst

Oriyome Fasuyi Olaifa Ekua Bobo Kobie

  for

                                                        otherwise

                                                the sure of verdict

                                        in the want of action

preserve the soon in afterwards

                        the time in africa

to jamaica

                                                    now the question

                                    falls

                            upon

            enemies

Zong! #21

is being is

or

should

is is

is

be

being

or

been

is was

is

should be

or

have been

is there

Ayodele Oluwa Oje Olayinka Motayo Babatunde

was

should

was not

should be

or

have been

is there is

or

being

there

is was

is is

should

and

have been

there is

was

there

_____

Ogunade Omotayo Yewande Abibola Sonubi Abeke

Zong! #22

    lives own their facts

             of spent lives

                murder

                market

           misfortunes

                    &

               policy

lying dead

under seas

         facts own their lives

in circumstance

        &

happening

               in trial &

declaration

             in the absolute

of rule

    &

lord

in the absolute

            of water

Muru Kakra Kolawole Kibibi Olabisi Usi

Zong! #23

was

    the weight in being

    the same in rains

    the ration in loss

    the proved in fact

    the within in is

    the sufficient in indictment

    the might have in existed

is

    the evidence in negroes

Zong! #24

evidence

        is
    sustenance
        is
    support
        is
    the law

the ship

        is
    the captain
        is
    the crew

perils

        is
    the trial
        is
    the rains
        is
    the seas
        is
    the currents

jamaica

        is
    tobago
        is
    islands

the case

        is
            murder

Kenyatta Mesi Nayo Yooku Ngena

is
justice

africa

is
the ground
is
negroes

evidence is
sustenance is
support is
the law is
the ship is
the captain is
the crew is
perils is
the trial is
the rains is
the seas is
currents is
jamaica is
tobago is
islands is
the case is
murder is
justice is
the ground is
africa is

negroes

was

Oluyemi Esugbayi Adubifa Ogunlesi Akua

Zong! #25

justify the could

        the captain &

        the crew

        the authorize

in captain

crew &

could

                could authorize justify

                        captain

  &

      crew

                        the

                        could

or justify authorize

        could

        captain & crew

                authorize

Bomani Yahya Modupe Jibowu Fayola

the crew

the captain &

the could

                                        the justify

                                              in

captain

                                              could &

                                              crew

                                      in authorize

justify

        the could

        the captain &

        the crew

                justify the authorize

                    the could

Zong! #26

was the cause was the remedy was the record was the argument
was the delay was the evidence was overboard was the not was the
cause was the was was the need was the case was the perils was the
want was the particular circumstance was the seas was the costs
was the could was the would was the policy was the loss was the
vessel was the rains was the order was the that was the this was the
necessity was the mistake was the captain was the crew was the
result was justified was the voyage was the water was the maps
was the weeks was the winds was the calms was the captain was
the seas was the rains was uncommon was the declaration was the
apprehension was the voyage was destroyed was thrown was the
question was the therefore was the this was the that was the
negroes was the cause

Omolara Chimaneya Adekemi Oke Mowunmi Iliola

DICTA

Zong! #

seas without
                    insurers
                    owners
                    perils
                    islands
                    africa

                                        owners without

africa
seas
insurers
islands
perils

                    africa without

                                        perils
                                        seas
                                        insurers
                                        islands
                                        owners

Zong! #

clear the law

of

order

cause

delay

of question

&

opinion

of the etc of negroes

the no is proved

_____

Zong! #

150sixtyfortytwoandahalfeleventhreesevenfiftythirtyseveneighteenseventeenonesix
weeks
months
weeks
days
months
days
weeks
months
weeks
months
weeks
negroes

was the bad made measure

Zong! #

islands
first
any
many
eighteen
other
three
particular

currents
any
many
eighteen
other
three
particular
first

winds
many
eighteen
other
three
particular
first
any

weeks
eighteen
other
three
particular
first
any
many

---

misfortunes

      other
      three
particular
      first
      any
      many
  eighteen

                           mistake s

                              three
                              particular
                              first
                              any
                              many
                              eighteen
                              other

              calms

        particular
        first
        any
        many
        eighteen
        other
        three

                           negroes

                              first
                              any
                              many
                              eighteen
                              other
                              three
                              particular
                              contrary

———————————

Zong! #

underwriters

of

perils

necessity

&

mortality

of

soon

only   &

afterwards

of was and

not &

them was

slaves

not

evidence

———————————————

Zong! #

uncommon case

great weight   new trial

great weight

new trial   uncommon case

new trial

uncommon case   great weight

uncommon weight

great trial   new case

great trial

new case   uncommon weight

---

new case

uncommon weight   great trial

uncommon trial

great case   new weight

great case

new weight   uncommon trial

new weight

uncommon trial   great case

Sal

Non enim erat tunc.
There was no then.

ST. AUGUSTINE

water parts

the *oba* sobs

there is

creed there is

fate there is

oh   oh oracle

there are

oh oh

ashes

over

ifá

ifá

ifá i

fá

fa

fa   fall

ing over

&

over the crew

touching there   is fate

there is

creed

there is

oh

oh

the *oba* sobs

again *ifá*   *ifá ifá i*

fá over   and over

the seven

seas   *ora*

in this time   *ora*

within   *ora ora*   time within

loss   *ora pro*

        this is but   an o

                    ration time   sands

the loss within   how many

            days how long   where being is

thirst & thirst   be being she   falls

            fortunes over   board rub

                            and rob her

now i lose   count i am   lord

        of loss visions   over and   over the *o*

    ba sobs   from there to   here bring them

                            no provisions   from is

            to wa   s sow

                    the seas

                        with she

                                    negroes ma

    n negroes murder   my lord

                    my liege lord

                                my *deus*

                        my us

        my we   my fate

my god   sun

                    der crew

        from captain   own

                    from slave

                                    under

    from

                            writer from

                mortality

                        mort

le mort le

mort le p tit mort

scent of mortality

she

falls

ifáifáifá

falling   to

port

over

&

over

my fortunes

a sin   you say

video video vide   *o* who says i am

the lord   of loss a rose

i say   a rose

for ruth   and for t

ruth sup   pose truth

then find

ing   a way

found   a port

a rule ought

evidence

suppose then t

ruth   a rose

over

&

over

with you

she f   alls falling

found   a rose fou

                    nd africa   un

            der water

                                        proved

justice   danger

        ous   the law

            a crime she

                    died es   es es

        oh   es

        oh oh   es es   oh

                es   s   o

                    s   s   o

                    s   s

                                o s

                    os

os

                    os

                                bone

    us us *os*

            save us *os*

        salve   & save

                                our souls tone

& turn the bo   nes

                        &

        salve   our souls u

s souls

            bo   ne souls

                    salve the slav

        e *salve* to

sin *salve*   slave *salve*

and *ave*   *ave*

    the rat the   rat *ave*

        ah we   cut cut

cut the   cost and serve   where s the cat

    the yam   no meat   trim

the loss   payment

    you say what   for where s

        the cat got

    the rat could

the crime out   out

cut the ear   be absolute do

    you hear

    the lute sound

to raise   the dead

    the died

    i hear

    ave bell s

ring   out

    dear ruth

    this is   a tale told

    cold a yarn

a story dear   dear ruth i

    woo time   and you do

    i have y our

ear   there were aster s

    at tea time éclairs   & you

    are my liege

lord of nig   nig &

    nog   my *doge*

    there are

stars in

sidera

as there is

ratio

in rations

but why ruth

do the stars   shine   if only

murder made us   you were by my side

os

os   *os*

bo   ne men

misfortunes

very new

and   we map

uncommon   the usual

to me   to the vessel   winds & currents

we ground   upon

i pen this

to you

when i am   her

able   paps her

dugs   her

teats

leak in necessity   there

was sin a good   supply of

ply the negroes   with

toys lure them

visions of l   ace for a queen

my queen

there is pus

dire visions

tempt all   night ride   me *dis moi*

do you

ruth   might you

and i   perils

notwithstanding we

seek the *ratio*   in africa negroes

too

de men   *dem cam fo mi*

for me for

yo for *je*

pour moi & *para*

mi flee

the fields   *gun bam*   *bam*

it was   oh oh

a falling

my fate

come to term   & murder

in lies   grounds justice

the noise   in lives

a discharge   him touch

ing might   you and i

ruth

oh the noise

nig nig nig   there was

zen in frenzy   & nog

nag

nag

all night

it is the age of guns

gin   & rum of

      murder   rimed with sin

                                    her sex

            open all   night rain

                  a seam of sin &

to market to market   tin

                                                    such

                        to trap a fat pig

            a fat nig   as never be

      fore seen

                        lords of reason

      all we were   a lace cap for my

            and sane men too   queen

                        sapphire too

      for my lady   gold

                  el son   a

                        song   at vespers

                              she rides

            my nights the   bell the good ship

                  vedic visions no

      gongs   provisions

                  niger sum nigra   *sum ego*

            sum i

                  am   yam   ben

am   am   gin

                        am rum make the mast

      teak men

                  who can cure

                                                    me the cur

      drag the seas   seven miles

seven   deep

    days

weeks   for *ius*   sing a song

     months   for us   of water

        for *os*   in bone

       for bone a deep

     wa   ter water

    deep bo

ne son   g to cradle

   her where the sun

      sink s

  under   throw them

    the rim   crusts lost   verses

     of sky circe   the seer

       appears

  lip s in rictus   there is an art

    to murder

with rant and curse   but the tense

      is all   wrong rum

   rain and more

  rum ah   but it s a rum

   tale ruth murder   & rum they sang &

        sang

      &

  she negroes   sang

mean   *le sang*

  red verses   groans *de men dem*

   cam fo mi

    here &   there

      a line   i

write   to

you   of

                              mortality s

          lien on l

     ife

                         on the

          ro

      se

                    on

          bo   ne   on

ne   groes

                                        such drab necessity

          murder

here we   re negroes

                                        like ants

          sow the sea   *is where*

we be   seed the seas

          with es &   oh & es   *os*

                                   &

     us

                    our pig got   with n

got   our nig too   egroes

                                   pai

     n captain pai   n

                                        tha

t hat   that hat

                         the rat mi lord

          my plea is negligence   to her i

               say *te amo*

her name   she smiles

        will be es   se to be   i smile

and i   am   fall

    am   falling

        am *sum*   into

    of all   murder

        am sum   am

    ame   if

            if

            if

    if only *ifá*

serve   the *oba*

        sobs again

    the tea men   there was piss *cum*

        let s have some   bile *cum* pus

            jam and   bread

    port too

                            & leaky

        teats   there was only

                bilge wat

        er for tea

            i argue my case

to you   take

        ruth   everything

            you must hear me   i say

        cum grano   *salis*

with a grain of   salt there was in

            surance again

    st sun   not sin

70

hum hum   hum him him

                          & him too

          a hero he was   and a negro

                                                      we dare

                    the deed

act the part   he cut

          the cards i won the   throw one

      deuce   two aces

                                      cut

              her

                                              open her

      shape   tie her

ripe   toes

          round

      and firm

                              the cord   it is

          dead she went   over &

                under she was

                                      wet put

              ashes

      on her water s

              leak oil   her and bring

                    her

          to me   no god

                    no i should

cut the cord of this   story

                    i rest

      my case   in negligence my plea

              ignorance *ave*   to *àse*

to *ilé ifè*   *salve*

to cain   to abel too

                                                        we need must

            meet with the east &

the west kings   be queens

            slaves too

        slip lip over   nip the rose   she spin s

                in the bud   once

                                                once

                                more

            falls   the *oba*

                        sobs

                again   & again the

                    tense the time

            is all

                                                wrong what will

                        mend

        my mind i cede   all good

                in the span of   pain

                    lisp my

    longing she falls   i will

                        loan   her

            to you ration   the yam and

                    the facts pain

        cap n pain   ma ma pat

            pat she s done   for

rêve master   *rêve* the she negro

            he s done for   drives me

                mad *je rêve je*   *rêve* him him

    him & him   her

too

din din

dong

aide moi i   ration the truth   the she negro

ruth   drives me mad

and the facts

whore they laid her

to rest she died

lave the slave   invest in

tin   in

rum   in

slaves   in

negroes serve   the preserve

the jam   and jamaica

rum i   remain god s jest

rimed

with sin rest   master rest we

have the ram   is it

just or just

us i *rêve* of   aster s

éclair s

and ruth   such a good

dog pat   pat nig

nig nig

nog

nag the man

ran the slave   ran ma

ma *mma ma*   *mai* bard sing

stir my thirst   for song a ruse

run ruth run

from me   & my sin mea

    sure the ease

         of

    over

    board   all

  fled the lair

     as if

    on wing   how

such a thin

    mite he

    was just

  seven

    de man him

cam   *fo mi a fez*

  pon his head row   row row the raft

  how *orí*

    orí   a gin nig

nig nig   *orí oh*   nig

   omi   *omi*

  nog &   *omi*

    oh   nag

  wa   wa

    ter *j ai*

soif she stirs   my   thirst

  an ace and

a deuce it was   pen my nig

  my pig then   they came

  for me *mes*

rêves our aim   to rid the good

  ship of dying   & death

of them

the way   broad & wide

as it was   long i won

her fair   the pig got

got to the east   & west over

the seas to sin   am i

a man   of wit

ruth i hear   you say

some see   the dove

on wing   the red   cove

le sang le   sing *le* song

le son el   *son* oh god no   hug

and tug *mai* she   ran *ma* he

ran *ma ba*   *ba iya* they   ran

the cat got gut

are we thugs   all gut   her

no no no   *run*   *run if you hear*

dogs hide the gods

are gone done

for hey

hola

run round &

round   sound of dog

of song there is   pus it rains

sin sip sup   and doze a dose

of the clap

suppose the hat

rode the rat round

and round   the fins

herd them   the crew does

my bid no sound   bell song lure

          her dong she   dives dong

     to the rim over   with you and   under she f

          alls falling   appears under

               water found   africa

          a rose   round

and round the hat   the rat

               the rot oh   the rot we

          sort them new

                                   rules state the test

               man for men

     & for t   ruth ask rome

          fist to the head mis   fortunes tune pain

               turn &

turn a   round the globe

          bill the bell

                                        & bell

     the cat she was   torn we sear

               & singe the rose

          of afric a mole

on her nape a bill   of sale flap

                         flap

          in the wind the sail   seal

the sale sad

                         sail s night   falls so far

          to afric & the dog

                              star

Ventus

The poet is the detective and the detective a poet.

THOMAS MOORE

sh h

not so

loud did nt the   bell ring oh

oh my

ass

hot   apes

all sing   sing

they sang *le*   *sang el*

song *le*   song sing

again   my goat bag of

palm wine

dance   dance they sing my

ass

lips gape oh   oh sad tune

sing again   they groan not

so loud

when did we decide   desire   *le sang*

pain   oh oh

they ma ma *mai*

with no

notes   tears they

sit *moi je*   am they

lie

over   them

the sun sow   the seven

seas

with   *aves*   of am

& ash sing   him *oba*

him

ask tiki tiki

fo me   the ship   heaves

sing i say   to

&

fro   groans

the *oba* sobs again   the din of my

own my very

own dying

negroes a pint

of gin the candle   flame s and a hey

hey ho once   an

am

died   dead

in its   sconce

he had an

ace   dear ruth

can a tale be

told

ever

i   held   a sequence

of

queens

one

king

tsuh chu

i

come

from

the north   the

dales   land

of mist

of hoar   frost

dear   ruth

there is

us

&

os

there is bone   *why does the*

shin bone shine so ruth

a secret race under

writers   lives of writ s

& rent s   cede

the truth

to the right

to be sure

this is   but

an oration

a tale

there is ruse   old

in insure

as

sin   is

new

circe

the crone

lips

a gape

sings

a

did we decide   tune

it rains writ s

piss   & bile

to the right   ran pus

         the truth

              & sin to be sure

                        tears

                             rum

                                  &

     why are we here

                             &

                                        where are

                    we   *we act the part but ration*
                                        dance   *the facts*

              dance

                        dance

         i say

              they sit

                                        they lie

                             i

     captain   their pain

                        wind

         strum s   the air

              he strums   the oud

                        the ship

     cradles   our longing

         our   lust   our

              loss   all

                   that is   old   in this

                        new   age

                   the time   the

                        date of

sin

                        clara

         that tune again

the air   it calms me

              but   then

         the   drum s

                   oh

the   drum s

     all night   they pray

         for   death

              shout   *lisa*

                   lisa

                        dear

         ruth   if

ora   a tale

    ora   be   told

81

ora   cold
         pray for me
                 & heave   men
heave   and
                 pass
         the peas   ignore
                 the pleas   omi
                                     omi
                         l eau
l eau
                         water   clair
                             the
                 sound
     of the oud
                         rouse s me
             the
     air   is
         danger   ous
             with
                             drum
sound
         i hear   them
     words   strange
             to my
     ear   the *oba* smiles
                 he has   *owó*
                     guineas
         cedis   too   i have
             guinea   negroes
                     they
     shed
             tears
         for   *ifá*
     ósun
             &
     ógún
                                     for
         efun
                     for
                 èsú
             ask for
     ame
             from
olú
     his eyes
 rage

would

bring   mi

me   run

to   death   from

if   field   de

he   man in de   hat

could   dem

she died   *cam fo*   mi

on   a tide   him

of red   *fun fun*

up river   *me ode*

where

we dare   *efun*

our *mortality by the*

desire   *tail*

at   dawn   *on the run*

if   if   if only

ifà

was   yak yak

yak yak

yam   pleas

my

own

she

negro

the

wonder

of   it

a   dower

gift   for

you

grain

in   the

field   sun

overhead

in

your

hair

gold   as

corn *first*

act   third scene

circe argues with eve

about eden   on the eve

of murder

rome mourns

her

misfortune

her

mort

her

p tit mort

turns

from

ruins

of forts

and   fortunes

to

found

a

city

on

death

on

murder circe

to eve

there is no   *writ in sand*

evidence of eden   *lives rent*

in eve eve   to circe   *lives*

i am

circe   the seer

sings a   tune a sad tune

with no no

tes *moi*   *je* am he

am she

am at last   *omi* water

l eau   *l eau*

il doge wears

a hat it is   red as is

his cape up

and

down up   and

down the wind

rose bail

bail & bail

water water the

wind   rose is wet

no

help *omi*

omi omi under

wind & up

wind we sail

with every

wind create a cat s   cradle on
                    the sea sing *te*

                                        deum s the bells
        the bells ding ding
                                and dong over
            the water done done   deed done died
                            done dead

there is fresh   fish no water
                rush rush feet
                        guns run red
                            run dear lisa
dave ask s this   is but
            an oration he   ask s that i
                        these words
come that i   write from his lips
        though my hand   shapes why
                are we here dear
                                clair i
                write   this
                        for
                    sam   who
                                is
                        by
                    my
                                side
                        there was
            ague   on
                    board
                                pus
                too dear eve
    piet says   he longs
                                        dear eva
                            davenport   i fear
                        the news   is
                            not   good
                    today at ten
at four   at
        six   &   at
                    seven   my hand
            writes
        we seal   the deal   the sale   of
                        negroes
                on   board   the
        sail
            slap   slap   in

85

                              the   wind
                    some
                         come   from   the fens
                    others   from the   dales
        and   the   far
                                          off   of
        africa i want   a
                              hat   of
              fur   for   you
                    ruth   shine   the
        negroes   for sale   the wig
              w ogs   the nig
                         nogs   get
              the   tongs   the
                         irons   hot
                    hot   sing
        sing   a   son
              g   of
                    sin   such
                         a
              din
                         such
                    a   ding
                    ding   dong
                         sing
                    he   sang
                         ba ba
                         iya
                                          mma
                              ma ma
                         the
                              raw
sea   some
        rush
                    nothing   but
              a raft
                         my once   queen
        now slave   there be
              no free   on
                    board
                         under
writers
                                   tire
        of writs
                    writ fine
              with sin

86

                    m lord
          the
            questions   can
                    we
                sin   within
                    the   law
                can   the
                    law
                                                sin sail
                                west
    then east
                            east
        then west
                        in   the hang
                            of
when did we   rope   there
decide   exists
hofi
            of pain
        such
                    that
                the
            poet   of
                the   trope
                    that is
                troy   can
            not   own
            but   there   is
                property   i
                    say
                                            in
                                    pope
                        in
                troy   in
                        rome
                    in
                                    negro
                                in
    guns
bam bam
                    our   eyes
            skim   the sea   for
    bodie s for   the law   in   *ius* in
            us   in
        os in   bone how
            many

did   you did
     i how
          many did   we
                sir what
         say you   no a
    queen
        once   now
     my
whore   to the crew
                    too
      are we but   bone
          men
            with
          out
    souls
        seed   to
      the   ever   in
          us   the
story   waits
         can   not   be
  told
        the *oba*
sobs
  again *act*
       scene m lord
    says the law
           is never
wrong can   never
    sin the negro
  asks   that i
   write
        a
    most   un
common negro he   hopes to re
      gain africa
  one day his   na
me is *wale*   he wants that
    they should wait
for him my eyes   rest where the sea
is   a   line a lace cap
    & red cape
with fur
  for my   once
   & nonce queen
          my she
negro make the mast

                              teak men   for
            flag nation
king & pope seek   the eyes hold   the hands tie
                                                                    the feet
                              the cut
            ran   from eye to
                  ear dear miss
                                                circe hans writes
            i ask   for your hand peter
piet   writes to miss clara   ted
                        to miss tara   asif to
      um   jon roy
                  & ned tom tim
                                          alf & jim
                              mike & dave
                  my crew
mates
        all
                  a mob rum gin   beer &
            cider
                  there was   grin
                        and gin   *a fortune in forts* *ahena*
                  gin and   *adwoa & danger*
                  grin round & round
the globe   we sail the sun s   *fifi*
            orb to   lead us if
            we can only gain   the is
                        land circe
      the seer
                                                pants
                                          waits
                              tempts with
                                    oracles
a trail of feet
                        in the sand
                              leads
            to the water   a
                  most un
                              common negro *you*
    take
                        pen you
            write
                              to
                  my sade   i
            play   a ruse   on
                  him

                    a trail of
                              lies
        lead to   my truth tame
            the rage   dance
                                              dance
                            i say *act*
                  scene my
    part is   set
            bring me my
      cape my
                        mask my past
                                        clap
                        clap i
          play   captain
                  pope   &
            king i   play
                              god
                    but
                              he s got the clap clap
                        men clap too
  limp
                                        to
            tup her do
                                        you take
                  this negro to be
                                    y our slave we
        make good
                                                time the wind
                                      is
                                  with us
                                      a   se
                        cret race
                                        we
                                    differ
                                      are
  we
                                          mad
                        or
          merely   men
                    without
        maps   in   an
                                      age
                  where
    truth   is rare   and
                              we   *dem cam fo me*
            dare   *de man in de fez*

not   his

eyes   a

his eyes   secret

rage   race

adzo   with

ama   a   taste

esi   for the she

negro & port pus

& ague they

faint sam   has a dose

of the clap too

and fine lace

for his

lady flip her over   & over

board was

a red dawn

they

were   drawn

down

ward

a re

ed   for   air

d

own

do

wn   dow

n   down

water

drag s

against

the grain

no   air

in   vain

then   they

were

ever

gone

divers   pour

les   *âmes*

nig   *les*   souls

nig

nog

nag

nag

pleas

air

fresh

air   *omi*

water   the

hag

circe   makes

a   ring

of   stones   in the sand

her o

mens have no

song

or

sound they   sing

of

the

pact

of   pain

be

tween

cain   & abel

bet

ween

ma

n

&

g   od they

sing they

dance i miss

the   city

ruth

tro odu

a pint   *fo*

of   *me*

beer   omi se o ore

you

say   ma

rk them

yes

let s

their   eyes

stare

such

fine   linen

my   lord

for   you

for   her

bod y   not

for   me

for   her

                                 my

      nonce

        my

once

              queen

         the   t

ruth

                in

         her

      eyes

        circe

      waits

        lips   hang

            make s

          fun

      of

                 eros

     of   us

          &

      ius makes

    pigs   of

     us

      bail

bail

    if

  you re   able

    or   abel

     dan

   and

sam

  saw

 it

        we

all

 saw it   why does the *oba* sob

  all day

it   ran

  rain

i

 long

   for   man

y   man

  negroes

   she

        negroes

      too

                                    for   sale
                                       fon
                                ewe

                        san
                lua   *& rada*
                            pla
                          y   man
                                    p
                          lay
        it s
                        an
                old
                            tune
            strum
                        it
                for
                        me
                all
                                day
                        a
                            tub
                        of   wa
                                ter
                            to
                share
                    let us
            claire
                        just
    us   just
                us
                &
                    ius
            slip
                    y our   lips
        over   these
                words
                an other   man
                        writes
                    in   the
                                    sack
                            of
                troy   the
                        rage
                    of   men
                                lives
                        the
                poet

94

writes

waits

for

the

past

to

part

for   the

red   sea

for   the

nation

inter   *pares*

for   the

city

of

g   od

with   no

go   d   spare

us

pater   *mon*

père

the   truth

ru   th cl

air ro

se

ev

e e   va

cla   ra sa

ra

co   ra ma

ry etc

all

wait

& wait

and

wait

& wait

for   a

ship

to

bring

their

men

to

them   *dem cam fo mi*

scent

of

                    cunt   &
                              ruth   he
                        dove   she
                                dove
                                            they
                              dove   omi
        omi
              oh   my go
                        d   they
                  were   go   ne
                    the   ne
                        groes
                              ever   claire
          the   dove   cote
where
          the   doves
                              nest
                  row
        row   slaves
              save   the
          boat   the
                        slaves   pig
                  got   got   nig
    got   got   in
        eden s   air
              deer   and
                    lion   cub
                will   lie
                        one
              with
                    the
                        other   we
                                    will   sail
                        to   the
                  end   to   eden
                    my   doe
                                    eye d   queen
                                        once
                                    &
                        nonce
                                now
              slave
                        ruth
                              read
                    this   sire
                      i will   rise

96

                              rise
                  say   the
            aves   &
            salves   the
                    meas
                    &
      culpa s   pray
                  pour
      les âmes   for
                              les
                  souls
            of   the
                              slaves
&
                        my own
      tie the
                        ram   *agbo master*
            to the   *agbo for*
      mast   men   *ori*
mon
            âme   *mon*
                âme   mo
                  name
                              my
                  name
                        we
sailed
                              up
                        the
            cunt   of
      africa   to
                              found
                        an
                  out
      caste
                        race
                  can t
      you   add
            a   market
                  waits
            it   fans   the
                  deed s   alms
                  for
      the   poet   of
troy
            for

97

          the poet   of
                  the   past
                     it   then   parts
        into   then
                     &
            now come
                     strum   the
                          lute
                  a   song
                     for   clara
         &   clair   for
            ruth   and
    sara
                                    how many
         did   i did
            you did   we
                  they   drum
                     a
    rude   sound how
                              they dance
                     always
            seek   the
                  eyes
         the bard   mourns
               piss   bile
                                          shit
               and   dung my
                  liege   lord   of
                     life of   death
                                    aide
                          moi ai
                     de mo   i aid
         e m   oi   thro
               dance   odu
                     dance   fo   me
    dance   omi   se   o ore
                     j ai faim   ma
    rk them   mark them mark   dem j ai
               faim j
         ai soif   dindin
               dong   dung
         don   din
            din   don   don   ding
    ding
       dong   done

Ratio

No one bears witness for the witness.

PAUL CELAN

shave me

now de   cant

the port   do you

                                    hear   him

pass   the peas

                              pleas

              all round   slap

                                        her slap slap

                                                              of

sail there   was only

        when not   if & ashes

to   seal this act   of

                        skin of sin

        of what a   deal my elation

                  ran

riot   my   seal

    on   a   deal

        well   done

    i   see   you   kate

                            clad

            in   fur   the

        ring   how   many

            carats

                              you ask

                forty   i

say ben   the lad   lay   dead

    mi   *omo*

                              mi   *omo* dear

              ruth this   is a

                    tale   told

    cold   an   old

                        tale   one

        note a   song an

                aria   for   clair

for   kate   for   clara

                    &   ruth
            etc   but
                        seal the
    sale   &   hear
        my   tale
                            told
            cold   sh h
                                    the
                    clarion
    sounds   for
        me   is it   a detail
                            man
                                        he was
                                of
            mien   hard
&   cold
    the   sobs oh
        the sobs   sam   was first
                mate the
                                                    oba
                sobs   again
                            omi se
        0   *ore*   over   and   over
                        again   this
                creed of   greed
                            is
        new   it   seeds   the
                the
                sea s   feeds   the
                        lust   for
                            tin   for
    gold
                    comes   to   rest
                        in   rest
                    rest   my   pet
                            my   she
                        negro
                            how do
            we   parse

                    the deed is   it one
          or

                        many how
          do   we
                    praise   the
          dead   a   job
                    well done   the
captain   says   the
          pain the
  pain *le pain le*   *pain el pan*   pant
                        pant &   paint
                            it do   i
                                            have your

                    ear i rave i
          rave i *rêve*   *je*
                rêve mes
  rêves
          les   *rêves* in   the e
                    den
          of   our gar
          den you   and i ruth will
                    have stag s   boar s &
          deer   carp in
                        the river doves
                there
will be dogs   fish   &
                        grouse   owls &
          tit s pea hen s too no   pigs he
          negroes   &she
negroes *je*   *rêve je*
                rêve pain has
          a lease on *mes*   *rêves*
                erase   this erase
                me*aveaveave*
slave save   the
          ave s save the   *salve s* the *vale s*
                too but not   the
          slaves   bilge
water

with scum

for tea bite   him *him*

        big man   him fun

fun   hey hey

                                        hey here's

                an oar row   row she rode

the roar the   awe of raw

        water *ba*   *ba iya*

                ifá one   day a clear

                        day it   was no

                mist in   the vale the dray

cart   the   hay clipclopclip

        clop you and i   rush

                & mud   huts we

                                    will

                rush the huts *let*

        we   *rush de cap n de*

                crew thud hold him

                                                lead her big

                with big

                                dat hat de fun

fun   *man* this

        is a sin we will   rush the

                captain the   crew

                                you ask

        me   i beg

                        dem fo   *ayo fo sade*

                fo

                                                mi omo fo mi

                pic kin the sun s

rays hot the gibes held   him led her the   negro rat

            a tat rat a   tat rat a

                tat tat dan jon &   will my   crew

mates good men   all who

            ever holds

                    the globe spills   the gore

dan is just   a lad *sit dem*

        seh dem   *eat beef*   *dem*

            have beer dem   *lav a*

                lav a the   shit the piss

& bile much ho

hum dear clair we

sat to

tea oily

beef and beer even

port some jam & spuds we

ate how do we praise

murder i

grieve my

fate my soul my late soul my

fortunes the loss of every thing every

truth my action a

sin no man can the awe of

one tear in a sea against the

hard reef of rea

son i

war with my

self *iya* *ba ba am beg you*

do ebo fo mi they

use their limb s

as oar s *je*

rêve je *rêve* is

it was it real master sir

me i *beg you you* *write fo mi you*

say ayo dem *cam fo mi in*

de field me run

run rat *a tat tat* if

ifa if *ifa* if

only *ifa oh*

les rêves erase

me clip clop clip

clop we act the part

most apt for murder i play

my part my past

my robe & gold orb *el orbe*

de oro my mask

if jim and if

jam am jam

am jam *lave*

l eau lave l eau   lave l eau je

                              me lave je

          me lave de sin   sure

                              as the sun any

sane man can   see no sin

        in the net of   our life our

                      lies bodie s   in situ in

              sand in   water geld

                              the negro now

      and wash the   water of all sin

              èsù   oh l eau

                  l eau wash

      the water   wash

              the water èsù oh   èsù

                      save

                              the   us

          in you the ius

                                          in us

no sin no   sane man can no   sane men au

              sein de in

                              the midst of gore

      de goré e sing

a song   for rose un

      son la son le   son for

                  rosa a san   man   for rose they

                      hoe   the field the toad

                              hops his ship   on

      the lip   of ruin her

              every where   his hip his

      sore toe   too   much   port rest

          rest rosa   a hero rosa

          says   is ever   alone

                              the deed must

              be done rest says   rosa me

      want fu   fu omi

                              water the dread   deed dare

d   & done drat   the cat dear

      ruth dear dear   ruth i   won her was

                  wont to   bed her bet

ten then   forty

                    guineas first an

ace

                    of spades the deuce   it was that

          got me her forty   days nights forty   times forty

sins can   a man   cede

                    his soul

          no she   won t at night   the rings

in   her nose her   ear s shine

     the perils of   ripe lips a firm

          form bare   ass skin *il doge*

               the laird my liege   lord

                         dives   amid

                    the din the

     dice the forty   *cedis* she bend s

               over the pain my

          god my   god why

                              olu seyi olu

     seyi hast   thou my son only

               a lad more   to me than tin

ore & gold *oh oh*   *omi omi*   *omi* oh me oh

          my god the cairn   *mei lua*

               mark s

     the place we   met the ferns

               where i hid the   rings ruth our

                    lips between cain

and abel a pact   of pain between

          her and me the   song *so la*

fa so   *la* far *isola*   *g long*

               g long   *g long*

     gong gong we ate   dates with rose   water the man

          in the red   fez and i   to

the east the   sun the dunes

               & gold

     tunis it is   a yarn i

          spin a tale   to be

               told not   heard nor

     read   a story that can

                    not be   un

told we were

a good   team sam

and me no   land no land no

more

land

for   the *san*

of the sand *me*

wale me   *king son run*

run save omo save

omo save omo omi

oh omi oh more

omi oh me   *beg* the vessel

rises it falls

the sea red

as wine rid   me of these

pests they   be

long to the   caste

of ants mis   taking gin

for water they mis   took

water for gin in *mi*   *tête*

pot is mi ju   *ju mi obi* re

verse the age   can we the

time the asp

appears the toad   hops the oracle

lives in the   omen the lisp

of *ave s* vesper   verses lap

lap lap lap

lap water cast   the net

wide for lies   to

found truth in the hand   s

pan of pain that

is s

pain a round

the globe *mi orbe*

de oro bring   the slop pail pin

her hold her

legs wide wet

her throw   water the shelves   a mess i

had an eye   a very good

eye   for   negroes i grade
       them only   the best   a runt here
                           or there the dog   star
          over us i   write i nod i
                write beg   god drown
                         my sin s in
rum reel about   the deck a raw
          deal weal s on her   skin they lash
                    her am spent
      now ruth can
                write no more salve   or raw skin *salve*
  salve slave she
                              reads & *ògún*   makes
                              men
      of iron ration   the beer &
                the amen s the veal   pies too
         & don t
                         serve gin to the pig
      the line   of negroes wend s
  its way to   the coast i saw
       a star the   dog star i set
            my path by   it i master
                    captain & there   is long ing
            for
the north for   the aster & for
                the rose sip   sipsip wa
     ter wa   ter
            omi lap lap mis   fortunes
                         rape this voyage   *mi*
  orí mi orí mi   *head ma*
     ma scene the same
                         sea ague gripe
            grips the   gut the gun
                              get the
         gun the man   runs she runs
hold them over
                    board with them   a rout it
       was a riot good   dog he   pats it *me*
            i be   *man me man*

me san me

lua   thugs all fins

    all round port   side star board

        fore & aft i am

against   sin shun crime   i must re

    sume my tale fins   all

                      round the guinea

negro pray s a name

                  a name what

        is his name he

  is *fon* he   says i re

    main man though   sin owns me the road

to rome is long   & my thirst

    for truth grow s *o*   *rí orí or*

i onise es   *o es es*   *o es* you

  my must now   my loss she

    has died coins   on her eyes cradle

the head linen for her   bod y ease my

    mind ruth she was   too thin hang

        him over

    board throw her   him too rum

more rum time   meet s truth in a pot

  of yam a

    song an ode   to the ne

gro in me in   you to the one

    the *son* the   song in

    negro i have   lost ruth round

and round sound   of guns they run

    dogs run to   ground not

    so not so

tups her then   tips her o

  ver in my gut   fear gut her them

    too the raven   nest s in *mes*

    rêves rome

mourns   her ruins her

  runes some mourn

    the dead we

        the facts the

lives *i*

lé i   *fè il*   *é ifè il*

  é ifè if   only *ilé*

    ifè we   led

                     them

        to the   rim o

       f life a sure   ruse & ruin

of insurers such   a loss such

      a sin we had   notes

         of payment *wa*

      àgbò wa àgbò

         wa   *àgbò* my

        son my son i

seek the oracle   of the

    owl we had scone s   for tea once

       seen the queen

   dies stone   scones hard

      dry we rescue   our tears

   from the sea se   cure them by writ *o*

ra ora o   *ra* pray rail   against time the

  age against pope

        & nation against   *l*

état the   state against flag

  for *òsun*

      fowl *iya*   *iya* m

a ma *ema* we   eat what

      is dead this

     story turns

tail runs   from the truth each

      word a stone

   to turn o

    ver &   over lose find

    & lose aga   in to fall from

my lips &   sink through

  the deep to the ruin   &

           rune

    of bone there are

suits there are   writs liens

  & notes le *mot*

just e the just   word just

a word *ave*   *ave* to

the negroes and

àse   the wonder her

sex wet we sail

west with   the wind then east

up the wind

desire me make   me make her i

will *i*   *lé ifè*

a vision we supped

veal with wine   here

is a rope hang

him *ora* pray oh

poet of try

& troy of trope

& rope her feet

un ange we fearing   the sea her feet

ran fore ran   aft fins fore

& aft negroes

fore negroes aft tap

tap stag

and deer such a grand   garden an eden

a stage from there   to

sing to the   stars *à ma*

santé à ta   *santé à vo*

tre santé   come a stirring

air a song a   tune sapphire ear

rings for you my

once my upon   a time queen   a lace

ruff too eyes   stare the fuse

of this

story his story

is long cuff

them africa s sap   runs free sop

to insurers soap

the negroes oil   & feed them with a grout

head for a captain

& daft   too louts for a

crew we sail

to the indies only   the owl s eyes can

see through the night

of this tale the noise oh   the noise gold

and sapphire for

you sue for me   a pension bone

of my bone song   of *le sang sang*

of my *sang* the last

to die are the eyes   we eat lotus up

and down up

and down he   strode trod

the board s as if   he owned

the ship i am in

orders i can pray   for their souls pray

for your own   master i pray this

is my due from goré e

they came to   spill upon the seas a dare

to the g

od s *n*

yame   *ò*

sun we   d

are you save   us

a rough band

of negroes   rush us mark

them her make   me mark me

too hot

tongs irons she s done

for where   my *ju*

ju iye ny   *ame* in an age

of rot dire

with peril &

danger why   are they why

is she here   why are we

in this tale this   story his story

save her i can

not salve her   sores i author

my own

fate *nommo* is   my

na   me

& my n

ame is   *nommo* is water

                        is word was

            a den a lair   of liars on

                        the ship that set

    sail where from   you ask africa

            i say how in   side the wind

clams feed on

                              weeds weeds feed

    on bodie s we wend   our way can

            you not hear the noise   ruth band of

    negroes run   to and fro ship

            sail ship   sail how many

                        men on board   ship sail

        ship sail how

                        many negroes over

            board her scent on   my fingers my hand

                        the scent of

    africa is with   me ever   on

            my skin my

                        lips your scent

    of rose s ruth   in

            my mind only   the rose s of war

do not last grow   sere we feed

            them *àse* then   feed the sea *àse*

        with them *àse*   bodie s limbs

                        a frenzy of *àse*

            fins round   and round *àse*   my gard

                en my eden   fish sup

                        on the g

            ore in goré e who   can save me

                        ruth how

                        can sane men when

truth is worn   thin my word

        is my truth now   drab

                                    faded of no

    worth we must   we must i shed

            my skin as does   the asp am

                        no more who   i was or am *san* s

skin raw with   out the sin

     of s

        kin in this age   of gin rum

    & guns this age   of *los negros les*

     nègres ignore the age   the rage of sane

men just   us ruth just

     us just *ius*   these are sad

days over me   *un ange noir*

       niger from the niger

    with wings do i   exist is it

     i i am ex

   man the sea   is now a bod y

pond and she   the one i   desire who arouses

    me an agent   of satan of

     lust is no   more i exit

la mer la   *mer* every

    where *mare* these   are sad days how

      many the ship

   appears a pig   sty sacks of corn

         & grain des

    troyed water   gone did we care

to spare them   their fate us   ours our fall

   they grow   wings

    des ailes   *las alas*

    we be   do *ebo*

for orí we be   use rum gin   some corn she

   is mine no   mine i had

one queen   the king   a two

   of spades   but she is my

    queen   my del

    ta queen   yo

      u spare *wale*

    sade & *ade fon*   *lua san ibo* & *e*

we we dis   covered them

   all man   negroes she

    negroes firm

lips put our mark s   on them hot

   irons raw   skin no cloud

    sun over

head *scene enter*   *il doge his red*

          robe parts we   ate cured beef

     & spuds   that night they hold

              her who won   her if only i

   had an ace wear   and tear of water

              on bone a short   stint on a ship

     a slave ship   was the lad s desire

              just shy of seven   teen there were for

tunes to lure   a man from sane

          to mad there   were perils pus

   and bile   he died   the lad

          ben of ague   told me he had   a

              girl with gold   hair blue

eyes and a   smile do you

     take this she   negro to be

          y our s

              lave y our queen

     bell the cat   there are rat s

          on board i do i   saw a sin so

              large

     as to make   you cry   & a man

          of you there is now

                   a lien on my

          soul

                   à

  se àse   of words

     & water carries   a ship yet drown s

          a man is not red   yet turn s to

   wine eats meat   on bones turn s

          bone into sand   were we u

          sed dupes   all to king   & state to pope

& *il doge*   to laird & lord

          but abel is   dead there is

     no bail for cain rise   rise sa

              lute the lust   for africa the sound

          of the lute stirs

   the air & my lust   for gold for

          guineas strum the lute   and

              sift the dunes of

tunis for the bones   the ruins of my
                story their s & y ours
                            our story it hides
        the secret that   in the rift between
                    cain & abel there
rome founds her   self on murder &
            on death come   strum the lute some
                    more for my late
        soul *sum*   *sum sum sum* i am
            sum i am i   am *sum* sum
                            of all ned
            s story no more
than eleven when   he ran a
                way to sea not   that far from the lisp
                    of ma
ma pa   pa he too had
        heard of a seam
                                        of gold so
                    broad & so
        wide in an age   of lust what
                are we
to do but lust
                                        let
                    us wed then ruth
            when the ship sets   me d
own on land   again and
                    be done i   am a new
        man sift the air   for enemies
            of my soul   they are many sh h
                    hush can you not
    hear the plea s   we were deaf to
            how to   mend this i am
god s agent here   on earth our rule   is
        just and   we
            must but   to err so far
        from reason   it is a leaky tale i
                recite it   holds no water with
    map and wind   rose and a lamp
            to see them   by we set
        sail crates   of portginwinebeercider   & water there were

spuds live   fowl pigs

even how long   have we been   gone

too long we are   lost this is

a tale with the s

ting of truth in   its tail on her

finger i tied   a ring made

from string for her   my queen *afra*

nigra she   throws it over

board has on her   finger a red

string for *san*   *go* she says

and dives

once   queen

regina smiles

and dives ruth pray   for me ruth pray s

for me i

pine for her i   fear to tell this

tale on the river   delta the niger

i saw a sa

ble skin so rare   i long to pet it

they grin be

fore they dive   or fall grin

and die all

of eleven and

dead ned he

too had the   ague we have

thrown him over

board we pray then   throw him pray

then throw   them pray then

throw pray then

throw pray for   us or them

what no seer could

do the winds   did they stop

us have been gone

too long   the captain him

self is at sea   with the will

in sure the how

in rule we set

sail with reason   only to lead

us to seek the   lure in for

                              tune to find

                                              only fear and who

                        we are flip

          her over flop   flop splash dive

                          dive my queen she

        dove on a wing   let me di

                  ve too   let me

                      die the hen

            ran the cat   ran the rat   ran the ne

                      groes ran the tongs

      the irons marry me   i beg

                    you there was   no hate no

          spite only   a job for a mad

                      king on his throne   rouse them all

    strip and oil   them this my song   of

              rage to an age   out side of time

                        where the sage live s

      the seer who see s   & does not

                    say it is   the age

        i tell you not   the man did

                    she falling find   a rose find a

                          frica under

            water a sad sound   the oud on

                          eid east   is west &

        west east where   sand meets the set   in sun there

                      we sang sad   songs sand

                          songs can you not

        hear the sound   of sand ruth

                      on bone we plant   the stems of ne

    groes in the seas   such a grand gard

                    en a red dawn   covers us

                          we will

        make the land groan   with grain and corn

                      dance with the sounds   of grouse dove s

                          and tits *enter*

        il doge he takes   *off his red*

                    cape puts on   *his sable one*

    the scene   *begins* we

              sail a boat   down the niger

                to the sea   port we have
    on board slaves   on the beach
              at dawn i   saw them the
                negroes clad only   in skin idle i
      stone the dog   what did they
            owe us nothing   round us the
                        earth groans   sobs
        groans again   with the weight
                    of rain i wait   for the blue
          night under   its cover i see
                her the *ange*
        the sable one   with wings
at first   light she is
            gone was it   fun only a for
    tune to be had   it had to
            be done at dawn   of day the dead
                    lay dead *in*   *situ* under
        water she tempt s
                            me spins
                a top falls ga
            ping apes all there   was a gap
in time be   tween then &
            now where this tale   exists *il doge*
                has got
                    the gout too
        much port he nods   he snores the tome
                falls parse
            the crime not   the sin parse
                & praise
        the negro who gives   us this day
                    our bread *le*
            sang le song   *el son* the deal was
        to begin   & end in
            time and we are out
                    of time lost like the
    ship it veers   from one
            side to the
                other i hear
        the sirens re   cite my verses they

lure me   on with my own
      words to wrap   me my only
            help the *moly* you   gave on the al
tar to my god a vase   of red rose s i fast
            i pray hone   my *mea*
                  culpa s my *te*
      deum s they rip her   garment her paps
                  hang dry she   falls we graft
      scions of africa in new   lands their sap
                                          ours i hold fast
            to my mind it slips
      falls in be   tween *aleph* and *beta* i
            lose it only   a gap
      ing hole where it
                        use d to be o poet
            of troy re   cite your verses i take
      my rum ne   at *à*
                  se àse the rain
            ran red they fled   the fields
the negroes we   ran after   them to the river
            only a reed   raft *san*
go oh hit her   over & o   ver with her loud
            sobs a mob bam   bam such
loss on a shelf
                        the mad king s calm
            bust stares   at me an urn *dan s*
                  ma chambre sur
      le lit on the eve   of the day i can't i
                  can my name i   have
lost   my name so much
            to gain his wiles in
duced us   me them the crew   *o*
      rí orí we sat   on the moss Ruth
            in the fen it was
      wet on the eve   of the day i left
            you *me i name*   *sade me wale*
me   *omi tola me i name*
                              ogun
      ba my iya   *she be*

queen my name   is

      ted is dave is jon   is tim is

alf is piet is peter

                ishansistomisjim

     issamisroyisdonisned   is mike is

esse is *posse*   is can ah but

    it s a rum

        tale not for yo u

ruth or yo u   clair or

     yo u rose or yo u

eve or yo u rosa   or yo u   clara

    yo u eva   yo u tara or

sue yo u   mary may mir yam

    or sara or yo u   yo u or

      yo u *scene il*   *doge*

dapper evil   *and rival to the king*

    appears exit

  the king i dare   you hold her

    over board make

      me never loud

cries loud   snores at tea that day

    he said we set

  sail to eden   and its end found

    only eve *afra*

nigra no   deer read this a

    sale of slaves thurs

  day oil them use   beef fat or

    lard *scene*   *the snores of il*

doge sire s   pare me what

    reason no sane man   should *de mans cam*

tek me we want fish   *for inle & corn*

  & sand the raven

      comes she wants

    my soul *mon*

  âme you have   my *cœur* she has

    my *cœur* the raven

soars i hear   voices she has

    my soul fear

  grips me my rictus   smile i hear

    voices *fa so*   *la fa*

so la fa   *me so la* she

                    calms me don t

you see is   she dead has she

                    gone we seek

        to tame them ta   me her

                                for me & for you

                    tame her we

        meet we mate   no need to wed

                        no meat no

    pan no *pain*   no no it can

                        t be a sin overboard   with you fish

            feed bit   by bit turn meat

to bone sea   fans def

        end the dead *orí o*

                    rí gbo mi   *mu* my queen she

    was but a toy   the story can   not stand the

                        t

            ruth only *el*   *son el son* my

                    song long   ago a tale was

    told with no   begin or end where

            s the port and what

                        my part come   men the gin

the rum read

                                        this ruth and die hey

                a pint of beer long ago

    a tale was told

                                            an ass and a twit

            he was

Ferrum

There was a noise and behold, a shaking . . . and the bones came together, bone to his bone . . . the sinews and flesh came upon them . . . and the skin covered them above . . . and the breath came into them . . . and they lived, and stood upon their feet.

EZEKIEL 37: 7, 8, 9, 10

Praesens de praeteritis.
The past is ever present.

ST. AUGUSTINE

                    me i   sing song
     for *ògún el*   *son* of   iron come bring
                                        our mask s
          let the play begin we   each act the part
                              in murder what   will they
                    how   do they the bones
          say what   cannot be give   voice to
                    a tale one   tale their tale
                    how bone be
                                                      come sand be
          come the tale   that can   not be
                    told in this   tale the *tao*
          the way of   the dead of   what do
                              es this mean drat
                    that rat it   ate the cat or is
     it the cat that   ate the rat halve
                    the ration of   cod the globe
                    spins a top of
          the possible help   help i can t it
                    is late t   oo lat   e the oracle
     where
                              lives the asp fore
     told the for   tunes and misfor
                    tunes how many   lashes sire as
                    many as you
     care to the bell   peals the gong
                    sound s *oraora*   *ora* pray i
                    beg you shave   them all over their
     head s their limbs   their arms oil
                    them the asp   crea
     ture of secrets writ   large slips from her
                    skin do not be   sad dear ruth
     you are   my muse my   must my
          can in my mind s   eye i see the
                    dales the glens   the asp
     leaves in the wind i   spy i spy
          with my aged   eye something that
                    begins with m they

are tense sweat   their fear weal s on

teats on arms   peat fires

in the bog be nice

to me i beg she   turns her

head her   lips from me i

slap her it s

only an   act a part

we play tears   sting my eyes i stub   my toe salute my

king the nation   the flag use the salve

to heal the skin can   we heal this

sin with salve *tais*   *toi* do

you hear a

bove or   is it un

der the roar   of

water their song *aide*   *moi aide*   *moi* help

me help me i   can t it is

late too late   the *oba* sobs

his loss *omi so*

o ore omi so o ore   water did a good

job me *ode* me   spear lion

and deer me

strong *ode* a tory   of great power bo

red me such that   i must gr

it my teeth

as if he did no   t he owns

ships though   on such a night

as this we dan   ce d under the st

ars you and i ruth they   dance too on bo

ard there is rot

in my toe & rot

in the age the scene   is my own no one

but i c

an play it i wish   a w

and to tempt   time turn it from now   to then while

it rains we   feast o

n flesh she rips and   tears

his cape does the news

stun you i am   cured for eve

r of good ask why

we sack their liv   es when last

i saw they we   re all stan

ding on deck his   cape is to   rn it

must be sew   n there is sc

ent of mus   k of negroes

where   s the pin

t pot of ale sin   g for me an aria

of   the asp oracle   of hope lord

and serf master   and slave god

and man you   and i all   meet in the no

de that is this   hip dear clair i

gnore this tale i must   recite all

the same they   suffered *omi o*

mio   *mi* o my go

d *o*   *mi* water if

ifá can if   *ifá* can

if only *i*

fá can all   that rema

ins are

words i do   not ow   n they t

read water   then they sin

k un

der the we   ight of *a*

men s ave s   *& salve s* the flag

falls a nation   mourns my fate

waits greets me

in what i   s to come a he

ro rose   up from a

mong the ne

groes *exit the me*   *n the king reads then*

doze s he hold

s a gold o   *rb in his right*

hand a b

ad brew this of unde   rwriters & loss there was

marry in greed

and profit they braved   the water get

the oar s there   was rush there

was roar there

was water arms   flail limbs   *un bras u*

n pied   fail him up   there a spear

in his side thur

sday is stud   day rut

    day the crew gets   up to antics

                me i be

         g you no   throw *ayo* sh

  e big   big *mi o*

      mo we can l   ease slaves ask

          the notary in t

    his time be   yond help we

fall to   our fate they

   to the o   cean their fate

      & grace hold   the candle up me

n so i can   see i mad

    e a rush   ring for you ruth

      wale make s a rush   ring for *s*

ade enter   *the kin*   *g he we*

   ar *s* red *r*   *obe with a g*

     old hasp s   o much s

  hit and b   ile and p

    us the tare s we   re in the fiel

d ruth *sad*   *e* makes a ree   d mat for *w*

   ale wale mak   es a hut of ru

 sh   and reed for *sa*   *de* the

                        stook s

  too & bog   rush *wale* will we

    d *sade* the dray   cart with ha

     y where we t

wo made o   ne the cairn

    where i le   ft a note

    for you ruth *wa*

   le is *sade s* kin   *g s*

ade is *wale s*   queen the o   men of *ifa*

has no voice   tar them kin

g at war with king   first tea with j   am buns *écl*

   airs bread an   d ham then

i will as   k for your h   and am i

    n a j   am j   im sort t

   hem one fro   m the o

ther hum hu   m shit pleas   to go

    d to rin   se the winds o

f per   ils make the sun san   e *de l eau* de   *l eau* wa

ter *o*   *mi* you say y   in me i pa

ou capta   u i he

y master o   ne cent for yo

ar the cri   es a fist ag

ainst he   ad a we

b of si   n traps m   e to sin

with such e   ase *wale*

and *sad*   e eat *fu*

fu den de fun   *fun dem c*   *am ba*

m ba   *m b*   *am d*

em *ha*   *ve bi*

g *gun* r   un *wa*   le ru

n run *s*   ade ru   n see *wal*

e run *sad*   e too at ves

per s i pr   ay no har   p or or

gan *pa*   ter *pat*

er j ai fa   *im* will no o   ne hear me

his so   n a spe

ar in his si   de thorns on his he

ad red stain   on his s

kin can he   turn s

our water bil   ge water into s   weet water g

eld him c   ut cut all re

d now her e   yes two lamps   in my very

own nig   ht we p

lay at dice   for the be

gin in new tim   e grows old

so do   es cir

ce the crone t   he hag the

seer a cast in her e   ye do

le out the bil   ge wat

er they do   le the water do

le out the a   le they do   le out the al

e we si   p port she la

y in   ert we   als on the sk

in no gar   ment to co

ver her o   r my si   n we sha   red her t

he king mak   es a dec   la

ration of w   ar so too the p

ope *il doge*   the laird t

he lord again   st *wa*

le and *sade*   there are o

mens in mis   for

tunes we sho   uld no

te *wale* a   nd *sade* w   ill ha

ve a   son *a*

de is his na   me the kin   g the p

ope *il doge* t   he laird and t

he lord mak   e a de

clara   tion of w

ar again   st him too *ori*   onise ada

aye ori ape   *re* if only o

mens lie   d you and i ruth w

ill have a so   n dan

te will b   e his nam

e slam her   head again

st the bo   ard s will

no one he   ar me b   ut dante po

et of the li   fe after death h   ear me o

h g   od ro   ugh winds

rip the we   ft of *wa*

le sad   e & ade th

ere are we   als on *wale s* s

kin *sade s*

& *ade s* too   *enter the kin*

g red ro   be gold th   orns on his he

ad a man ge   lid as the north   he

comes from if   we cede the is

les to the kin   g of spa

in what have we w   here can *wa*

le and *sade* hid   e in time in

the p   ast can ca

in can cai   n can & did d

o a

bel cain c   an cain ca

n & ab   el is not a y   arn a t

ale a sto   ry that can

t can co   me eat sip

and su   p at this tal

e that can t c an a sa

d tale it is i ran t i ran

t run fro m the sun s rays i am h

am h am i a

m i a m cur se o

f go d by g od cur

se d as they are h is so

ns of nig ht thr

ow n out side of ti

me ha m i am that

i a

m do not be c oy with me

ruth i b eg you *let*

us have a ne *w act a new s*

cene new a *ct new sce*

ne so here is dido she

discove red the save

in africa find s a hid

e found s a city again

st ro

me and the vise

of time *w* *ale* and *s*

ade g row g

rain to ma ke beer *the kin*

g sits on his da *is on his is*

land read s a pa

per tha *t says he o*

wn s negro *es man*

y man *y man* *y negroes* we din e on

egg drop so up eat fish

roe fe ast on dat es from

the e ast cure

d ham & beef the ne gro serves fresh p

ears on a tray

with my pro fits ruth

we can ma ke gin

with the g rain in our fie

lds circe and her sire ns sin

g their son gs tempt wit h all t

here is to eat the *san* can sin

g they dance   too haw   ham i

s where i   live a sad s   ad land this i

s land where ti   me sag s wh   ere i sail fro

m to serve m   y kin

g you al   so serve rut

h who sit s   and wa

its on time how l   ife fli

es we we   re ma

king gain   from the   m to sin

k all we had in s

kin le

g irons   on hi

m her too i want   you to li

ve in e   ase ruth cl   air cla

ra ro   sa etc where

meet *a*   *leph* and the o

m in o m   y god my

god a he   ro a

rose a sh   e rose we   must cure the

m of a   frica w

here be

gins the lon   g in g   one where o

ld and n   ew are but

words our fort   unes are   at s

take the ship   glide s m   ist all

round *les nègres*   *sont gens pas*

thin

gs *pas co*   *sa s pas pas*

the loan of his

pani   *ola to the king*

has gone

bad me *o oni*

me be kin   g me i

as   k you sp

are *iya omo*   me i   pa

y gui   nea for *omo*   me i sa

ve the   m *je rêve j*   e *rêve i*

l rêve do   you *rêve* ru   th

beg

in where it   be

gins there i   s no such   where he

            i only   tell a sto

ry it c   an not be tol

            d *dem gi*   *ve tiki tiki fo*

    ini fo tai   *tu fo ma*   *i*

    t   he king en   ters gold on his he

            ad the cre   st on his se

    al is g   *old* the see

            r peer s into ti   me to come sees no

thing sees only   time to come *isola*

        i so la mi   *so la mi fa*

        so la so   *la* this i

    s how the so   ng go   es where the

bee suc   ks there   do the s

        ums ma   n fifty ne

    groes   take away ten   leaves how man

        y *cedis* her   in my l   ap a g

irl betwe   en lisp and s   lip the slip

    of his ro   be red we s   lip them st

        em from roo   t pare them d

            own for a gar

        den never see   n where be

gins the eve   r in ti

    me the bell sounds   gon go

            ndo n do n they   give us s

    lip are go   ne be

        fore we ca   n say o

    ver wit   h you the s   um of six

        ty & for   ty is ze   ro cir

        ce the cro   ne s

            it s a   top a pi

            le of bones

    me *o oni* m   e king yo   u kin

        g we be   ki

ng you sp   are *omo mi so*   *la iso*   *la*

mi   *isola m*   *on ile je rê*

    vejerêvejerêvede   r

        uth *the k*   *in*   *g wa*

nts to   *ma*   *ke*

        lo   *an of*   *his pan*

i   ola h   e holds

t   he has   p o   f his ca

pe   h   is g   old o

rb   h   er in m

y lap sk   im the s

kin of the se   a *la*   mer ma mer

el mar ma   *mère mare*   for e

yes l   egs ea   rs h

ands hea   ds & f   eet f

or bo   die s l   im

bs for ri   bs spin   e s to

es shi   n s & lip   s for pel

vis   & fe   mur

for   mo   lars f

or *ho*   la &

hey *ave* &

sa   l   *ve* for i

c   a   n   i can for i

am *je*   *suis & yo*   *so*

y

for *sum*   e   go & *eu*

sou scan   the se   a the w

inds for the ta

te te ta ta for tum   de tum for

a be

at *o*   *bi obì mi*

o

bì ifin sa   ve me na   ils in his p

alms nails   in he   rs red *fa*

so

la mi

so la re   *mi so la fa mi*   *from i*

le ifè m   *i from o*   *ya olú*

fe   *mi o*   *lú*

seyi skin   kin

g &   queen of kin   we

t her tie   her by the h

eel her nails   ra

ke my s   kin she s

pit s s how did w   e get in

to this me   ss *act s*

                    cene anger

        mark s the kin

                        g s mien his an

        ger is dan   ge   *rous we must*

have ca   re they lie   on shel

        ves logs   tied one   to the other oh

              the sin of i   t all hush can

        not let t   hem hear me ru

                    th spin

    the globe turn   it un

                    der your h   and see how f

              ar we have   go   ne scan

              the wa   ter for *el*   *pa*

    n de vi   *ta* bread   of li

        fe fo   r bo   nes to   e bon

e he   el b   one l   eg bo

        ne hi   p bo   ne ha   nd b

one a   rm bon

        e no   se bo   ne e

              ar b   one fin   g

        er bon   e hea

                    d bo   ne bon

        e bone all   is bo   ne wha   t be t

                    he be

        at in b   one how

                    say the o

    racle bones *eyo*   ba eyo ba   ah eah

        lo ong o   ba ka

              ka serah   foh

              la ahpa serah foh

egon egon sura   *sha* there

              is be   at in bone

                    the   re is go

ne in bo   ne you wish   to wed e

        sau a dower gi   ft for you gr

              ace a fine she   negro now i no

    d my eye   s drown dow

              n down dr   own the won

der the *wun*   *der* of under wa

ter what ra   ce of me

            n this ni   g nogs   of guin

ea how man   y guineas   for this gui

        nea man once the   re was on   ce up

on a ti   me *il*   *y a hay*

                            & *est* ro

    me tro   y & si

                        on there was

            on   ce now she

re   ad s rapt th   is story

        yarn a tale   which w

            ill not be   told yet w   ill have it

s say it   is a wh   ore age w

        here all li   ve by evil how   ca

            n we ye   t we do we

    grip   e we gr   in we grie

        ve the   n gr   in a

            gain fez   lives aga

        in in   the m   in

                        d and the *o*

        oni of *oni*   *se* rides int

                o war for   neg

            roes for sla   ves how man

y *rotls* f   or this guine   a man he

        asks we eat pi

                            g pies por   k with sage

            and sion so   me port she

    reads no   mo   re of the a

        ge of ho   w wh

            y & whe

        refore of who   res who   serve

                                                    tim

    e & pee   r into t   he past   at ves

        pers tho   ugh they sin

g of nigs   and of no   gs and s

    in hey herb   cast of   f the gri

        pe s hans cut   the rope s scion s

of ro   se and ye

    w of af   rica we had

        with us s   lip s to gar

den with the tin

es of ti   me grip th   e past w

   ill not let   it go   or me

be nor will

  i o   ver the se   a amen s of ves

   pers rin   g out & o

ver cries o

     ver sho   uld o

   ver could   and no o

  ver & ov   er & o   ver miss cir

   ce takes a sci   on of the herb si   on

with so

     me sage *pate*   *r* i wi

  ll lift mi   ne eyes *sin*   *me sin m*

   e sin me with   out me sin

   g the vesper ver   ses ring the

  m out loud o

     ver the wat

   er *il doge sci*   on

o

  f rome sin   *gs at ve*   *spe*

   rs of n   *igs and n*   *ogs* there

was

   ague the   re wa

     s grip

  e there w   as fren   zy th

   ere was e   vil there   was a

  men a   nd *a*   *ve* there was *me*

   a & cul   *pa* t   he

   re was gr   ieve & wo   e

  si   n th   ere w   as

no

   is   e of neg   roes oh th

   e no   is   e there wa

  s pro   fit the   re was

   loss there   was ga

  in t   heir loss

     ayo

  do ague   *fo mi* who   wh

o ho   o h   oo o   men o

          f   owl & a   sp *ye*

ya ye
                    ya ye ya   *ah y*   *e ye ye*
ye ah ye   *ye* i ro   de the ma
          re to me   et you th   at da
              y on the da   le fi   sh sup a
     fin   ger her   e a le
          g there ma   ke the   ir ho
              me in bone o   racle bones ah   wo o
     ah wa ah   wo wh   ere is *wa*
          le sa   *de* too a
              nd *a*   *de* whe
     re the hu   t of ru   sh ree
          d and red   mud w
              here the ree   d mat *sade* ma
     ke s for *wa*   *le* who car   es for *a*
          de now &   then *a ah who*
              o ai ye ee wh   at is the ti
     me where be   the be
          at in bone sir   en s call t
              empt with son   g all night
     a stir   ring son
          g to mak   e my lo   ins sti
              ff har   d with de   sire to fi
     re my lust   the sir   en s song
          fa s   *o la l*   *a la m*
     i fa   *so r*   *e re d*   *o do mi*
          f   *a so so la*   *do* on bo
              ard we ha   d spu   ds win   e por
t ru   m ha   m corn & rice   i have to
     ld you a   ll that be   fore & wa
          ter
to se   cure our pro
     fit we th   row them to res   cue our for
          tunes we   do mur t   hey f
all to in   sure our pr   ofits ov
          er & o   ver a   gain to sec
              ure their re   scue the   y fall o
ver bo   ard to pre   serve our profit
     what i   s bo   ne bu

t bone stone   of then evi   dence of a pa

st drow   ned in no   w p

lay on my bo   nes the son

g of bo   ne in b   one sh h ca

n you he   ar the be   at in bone *pie*

je

su pi   e *jes*   *u sanctus santuc*   *sanctus ag*

nu s dei in   *san*   *ctus* there i

s *san* say   a *sa*   *nctus* for m

e a *san*

ctus to the s   ea a *s*

anctus to the s   *an san*   s *san s*

san s s   *anctus* i

am we a   re their e

yes stare   see thin   gs we ne

ver wil   l let my s   tory my tal

e my g   est gift ri

se up in ti   me to sn

ap the sp   ine of tim   e *pat*

er pa   *ter* say a *pie je*

su for me   add a *s*   *anctus* th

row in an *ag*   *nu s dei p*

ater for me a *mi*

sa una m   *isa* how man

y gu   ineas for a *mis*

a pate

r prat   e the *a*

ve ma   *ri a* pra

y *pa*   *ter* pray f   or me

for th   em sa   y a *san*

ctus f   or the s   ea but dr

own the can   t *pater* i   t is do   ne lots

of *pi*   *etas* to   o *pa*

ter

& *fi*

des & sp   *es* dum d

um de du   m dum th   e no

ise the   noi   se th

e drum it do   es not sto

p the *o*   *ba* so   bs a

gain what d   eed this

     hat cree   d have we cre

ated in our nati   on of cards   we sa

     il the se   as to the e

ast sat   in the we   st the in

    dies go   ld and t   in she s

      erve s us a d   ish of s   puds wit

        h so   me sage

& a sci   on of the her   b sion o

  ut of the d   eep *p*   *ie jesu*

    pi   *e je*

   su our cr   eed of no no

t & new b   less me *pat*

   er i a   m sin *o*

rí o   *rí or*   *i o*   *ni*

 se they   hug the   y fa

  ll *la* m   *er ma mer m*   *a mèr*

e wh   ere does di   do fl

  ee to a   frica what do   es she ther

   e she fo   unds a cit

y why do   es did   o flee she see

   ks a pla   ce to rest   an a

    cre of ho   pe in a hide

     where is d   ido g

one to g   round in afri

    ca *wa*   *le* and *sade* u

     sed to li

   ve in af   rica did

    o flees to afric   a seeks a

place to re

   st an a   cre of hop

e in a hi   de to f   ound and g

   round a c   ity hip h   op hi

    p ho   p the to

     ad ho   ps its pa

  te bare a r   uby in its l   ips it i

   s a story i   cy c

    old in i   ts de   ep s th

  eir eyes star   e at u   s how m

any s   uns are there i   see si

                    x me i h   ave ten s

        ons me big   man me   asure the r

              um & the lo   ss in   o

                    s in u

    s in i   us the s   hip veers to t

        he west e   ver what d

              o the bones   say ru

    th the r   eed the ree   d us

        e the reed   for a

              ir ma   re m

              are all i   s mare a

                    ll is se

              a the   y quit ho

        ld of the ro   pe fa

    ll & s   o qu   it this li

        fe par   e the spu

              ds a   nd sp

        are the ser   mon s tie

    the fee   t se   w the ey   es sh

        ut it i   s do   ne cap

              tain d

              rap   e the tor

    so the li   mbs wi   th li

        nen in my e

    den the   re is do   ve t   it and rave

        n ow   l too th   e ease

        of i   t all t

        he crew i   s no   t sa

    d nor the c   apta   in a to

        ad by ano   ther name i   s un an

        ge a rub   y in he

              r lips the su   n s dis

    c hang s r   ed & ho   t ove

        r us th   e sa   me ru

        se the sa   me m

              use you h   ow it gr

    ow s the f   ear we hu

        nt eat har   e in my ede

    n we hun   t them t   hey eat th

              ey shit i pla   ce my wi

                                                            143

g on my he   ad they e   at they s

hit my lo   rd my li   ege lord i sa

lute you w   e sit o   n the ru

g a go   od rug fr   om the e

ast from t   unis eat dat   es fresh f

igs mak   e musi   c with ou

d and tars ma   ke de   als for ne

groes with the m   an in the re

d fez fr   om over th

e gold dun

es rut

h my m   use i lo   ng for y

ou to hu   g me to   w row r

o   w row r   ow r

ow to   ad and t   it mo

use in m   y e   den o

rí o   *rí me b*

e thir   *st* reams of no   tes for y

ou to so

rt tend the m   are the toa   d hops o

f f into the n   ight drops its r

uby pen the p   ig pen the n

ig sing a   n o

de to ni   ght & to the s

in un   der the s   kin to s

ion nig   ht s vo

ice i   s wit

hout so   und the s   un ve

ers we a   re out s   ide of time and o

ut of ti   me dar

e to step f   rom trut

h to wad   e in de   ath in d

ying and di   do flees her fat

e to a   fri

ca finds i   t their fa   te o

urs ru   n to grou

nd their f

all our f

all i   t was a b

ull marke   t for g

uineas & gui   nea negro
es a b   ear mark
            et in h
ope nig   ht fad   es to da
      y da   y to n
            ight her d   ugs ha   ng sa
cks of d   ry fe   ar ho   pe fad
      es to fe   ar th   ey eat t
            heir fea   r and all   roun
      d is f   ear i mo
urn you mo   urn we mou   rn our *mo*
      rt they hur   t we w
ill have a big d   ish of s   puds with b   eef *el s*
      on the s   ong we e   at we d
            oze she but a b   it a s   lip of a g
irl we c   ome to p   raise the r
      use in d   upe they pr   aise *o*
rí i   *lé i*   *fé* in a   n age so
      rare that p   hrase again the   *oba* so
            bs with pra   ise and p   us the sh
ip sail s o   n board s   aint sow & ca
      ptain p   ig s   aint s
            in & lor   d tin the v   essel y
aw s first e   ast then we   st i p
      ray to the e   ast the   n to the w
est to the n   orth & so   uth no e   vide
      nce of g   od but o   ur negro
            es have ya   w s the y
      aw s le   ak p   us
there is n   o new t
            hing here on e   arth *de fun*
      fun m   *an come t*
ek we a   *way* we li   ve by old cr
      eed s ma   de new the   more to su
            it our de   ed s have the r
am tup the e   we i tup & t   op the q
      ueen of s   pade s in our ede   n the pi
            g grouts r   outs in the d
ung we sa   il we
      st for e   ast & e

den the capta   in a man o
f girth of har   sh mien and vo   ice eve
          n with the s   he ne
groes i s   aw him r   ub his s
        ex aga   inst her i se   ek no g
            old no   r tin no sap
tin sap   phire no   r rub
        y nor the o   re of the i   ndies m
            y eden is y   ou r
uth only y   ou *me i b*   *e od*
        e mo   *i je suis*   *ode* we ca
            me d   own the r
iver the   re was a f   ort in the mi
        st wh   ere we wo
            uld prove our mu   st our mig
ht & rig   ht there wa   s dew o
        n the   ir ski
            n on he   r sk
in he wa   s a sly o
        ne with our guine   as we turn t
            o the or   acle it tun
es our fort   unes wh
        ere must cre   ates will th   ere ò
gún live   s a twi   t and a l
        out to boo   t he pas
            sed out o   n deck a
pes all th   ey shed t
        ears fresh t   ears will not e
    at sal   t will never s
            ee a   frica aga
        in they s   ay a s   cene neve
r seen b   efore & w
        e are late in t   ime for the e
            ast ede   n & eve
r *wal*   *e and s*   *ade* have no   hut i ca
    n not b   ear this t   ale told b
        are of all t   ruth ru   th you a
re my m   ust m   y can t
            his story i   s not mi
        ine to t   ell tell i   t i m

ust it was on   ly trade after a

ll *act s*   *ix sce*   ne o

ne we mat   e them a b

ill of s   ale for a b

ale of h   ay a gu   inea m

an a ne   gro *my fri*

end i p   *en this to y*

ou since y   *ou are my f*   *riend an*

d will no   *t* we fish for c

arp in the ri   ver ferns all r

ound *i w*   *ill eve*   *r brood on e*

vents seen b   *y me* to give m

y me all to t   he nation b

ut i was cu   red of my l

ust for the s   he ne

gro they han   g on

with tw   o hand   s we t

ug they f   all f

orm un f   orms hal   f man hal

f ape h   alf man a   ll a

pe *i*   *fá if*   *á if*

á if o   nly *i*   *f*

á

after the r   am t

ups the e   we tie i   t to t

he mast o   n d   eck *àgb*

ò for *ò*   *sun* the bo   ard s ran r

ed from the r   am *le s*   *ang* for *òs*

un sin   g sin   g si

ng th   ey sing *fa f*   *a fa* i

f only *if*   *á* they li   ft the bo

die s ma   ke an a   ltar to *ò*

sun to s   *ango* we s   ing our *a*

ve s & s   *alve s* t

hat phr   ase a   gain the *o*

ba sobs *s*   *ame act di*

fferent s   *cene* they dr   owned *il d*

oge p   reens his to   e so

re with g   out the mo

ss on the s   tone where we s

it you a nd i rut

h and eat a d ish of whe y we s

ail lead in t he sail from a frica s c

oast to ow n now never eve

r & w ill we sa il for a far is

land for sunsh ine se a do

gs in a wo rld of wa ter the wo

nder of i t all in h

ope that we le ave sin the sta

in of ni

g and no g is with u s ever *d*

iff *erent act sa* *me sce*

ne they dro wned the *ob* *a* sobs a

gain & a gain that ph

rase god ch arge s us w ith their we

ll be ing will he c

harge us with a c rime *i*

lé ife li ves no quest ion s at s

unrise or at the f all of the s

un the sun veer s then q

uits *u*

se her as y *ou w* *ill she is n*

ow y *our s* *sin* s

in i a m wit

hout sin b ut we me et be

come friend s sea fa

ns dance se a cre

atu res ride the b

ones we rest they re sist the r

am is dead *no res* *cue to*

day seas e *alm* sam calms

her wipes her tears the

se creat ures a se

cret race a qu

est so di re i fe

ar the e nd t

roy but a r uin a ru

ne a secret s ure and se

cure on th is day i quest ion the rise

in sun long for night the candle

in its sc   once shows me   the way to her *que*

     es esto what   is this wha

          t do   es this me

                         an my ha

nd writ   es the rea   son his h

     and writ   es the reas

          on a pin   t of be

     er some por   t to rin

          se my s   oul of s

in can a b   at swim a s   in die the

     y had mort   ality by the t

          ail in did   o afric

                    a grafts r

          ome to her a s   ecret so se

               cret the b

ill was d   ue the no

     te wa   s due sh   e was du

     e o   verbo   ard wa

          s no mo   re *la*

d on the q   *nay wan*   *ts to se*   *t sail for t*

     he ever in e   *den does not s*   *ce all tha*

t waits for h   *im* fe   aring f   ear they

     and we g   round on the re

          ef of o   ur st

ory ear   rings o

     f sapp   hire fo   r my g

          irl rub   y too fea

ring her e   yes i run   her fe

     et co   me af   ne enemi

          ter me mi   ne enemi

     es set upo

               n me *il*   *é if*

é an e   gg for *ò*   *sun* it i

     s hot in her   e piles & he   aps of fin

          ger ring s n   ose rin

g s ear r   ing s the cre

     w shares we din   e on me

          at sip win   e *à ta san*

té dear r

               uth *ma chè*

re ruth a fe   ast we had *mis*

e en scè   *ne*   a shi

                        p or v   esse

l the s   ea man

                y negroes a ran

t of rains the   y ring they sin

                g they b   eat u

                        pon the d   eck ho

        ld the e   ar ring fast bo   y *so*

        me neg   *roes had pil*

                es leaky pile   *s* the saint of tro

        y and the de   ad city ro

                        me app   ears to me

at night *l ang*   *e de me*   *r noir nig*

                er afer her s   ex we

        t her p   aps leak p   rop them u

                p *ilé*   *ifè i*   *lé if*

è il   *é ifè* se   w the lin

        en slip sh   ut we ro   t in this ves

                sel from s   in sin

        g by rot   e a stir   ring son

                g their dy   ing grist & g   ift to u

                        s *tō se*   *cure a pro*

        fit we u   *se man*   *y ruse s*t

                heir swe   at the sce

                        nt we stu   n the su

n with o   ur act it

                veers off i   ts way we

                        let win   ter s frost fr

om her urn no *a*   *ve s* or *sal*

                ve s only sla   ves *às*

                        e àse so b

                e it the so   und of the o

        ud on e   id fa

                        lls on u   s on tu

nis a st   ring of n   egroes on t

        he qu   ay no sou   nd the m

                an from f   ez wa

                        its to se   ll to ma

        ke a de   al *the sti*

ng of t   *ruth is e*

ver with m   *e i ma*   *he y*

ou a g   *ift de*

ar ru   *th of th*   *is she ne*

gro her na   *me is sa*   *de i cal l*

her di   *do u*   *se her as y*

ou u   *ill*re

ad the poe   t of t   rope t

roy & r   o

me *wa*   *le* and *s*

ade ma

ke   grist to b   rew b

eer whe   re r

iver me   ets se

a meets p   ort there stand

s a f   ort of n   egro

es the men w   ear no p

ants the sh

e negro   es have bar

e t   eats a m   ist co

ver s the fo   rt on the riv

er on the po   rt a l

ace ru   ff for my neg

ro and sat   in pants t

oo i mak   e you a g

ift of hi   m they p

ant they fa   int to plan

t a fla   g for na   tion & for k

ing to p   lant our s   eed my to

y for   t sits on a r   iver on a po

rt i p   lay at gun

s no s   lave s fire   no shot s

in nest s with

in come sir   my lie

ge lord it i

s now y   our turn co

me b   e me rains fa

ll no wa   ter in the tub   p

lay your p

art the sun rose

under sk

in sin for   ty days fo

rty nigh   ts forty *ce*   *dis* for forty

sins *j ai*   *faim j ai*

faim god of   spire *spes* and p

raise turn and   turn the bo   nes sing

a son   g of wa

ter a wat   er so

ng sin   g song sin   g song de

fend the d   ead & sin n

o sin sin   g the bo   nes h o

me what w   ill my b   ones say h

ow do the   y forty we

eks come to t   erm sh h *au*   *di* can you

not he   ar from the de

ep s the voi

ces not sir   ens we are a

t sea the d   art of my sto

ry stings i me

ant no harm   no hurt res

cue us rag   and bone men in

dict the a   ge pears in g

in in   wine win   ter wine and y

ou ruth   this story ne

sts in the ne   t the we   b of ti

me tam   p it down do

use the flam   e of this ta

le what pro   fit me if *mon*   *coeur non est*

we wind o   ur way sub   wa

ter thro   ugh bon   e bed s o

nly the bone   s of the sh

ip their e   yes dart this

way and th   at soft so

ft they ro

am the ship   their cri

es grate on m

y ears drag   the dee

p s for the b   ones of my so

ul their sou   ls cast the n

et wide to the d   eep men to the dee p and a   tot of ru

          m for y   ou scu

                m upon a ti   me at the be

  gin in nil   e the bl

          ue nile a lin   e of ne

                  groes gain t   he shore w

  ill the sea   give up its de

            ad its bo   nes cob s of co

                  rn sacks of g

      rain by gra   ce and by lar

            d *père* grant u   s this da

                  y our n

ig nig no   g and so

          up a rash of s   in it was hang

                him overb

      oard throw h   er never se

            en again mar   ry time to t

                  ruth you t

    o me ruth the d   un horse wa

                its under the t

          ree for u   s cede the l

and grant us w   rits *il doge* be

            deuced they p   ray into wat

                  er what was d

            ue them but   life i

  t self they wr   their c

        rie s their gro   ans their sob

              s their oh s th   eir ahs ya

  weh what was s

                              he worth *esta be*

          lo lindo my *geld*   *is op my mon*

    ey spent she   is y ou

                rs they ar   gue water fle

    d water al   ms and arms fo

          r the poet of t   roy of the past

  that is no and   now who writes o

              n water this po

        em of lo   ss the shape of th

              is now b   ones to sand t

o clam s the tr   ope that is tro

y is *de tro*   *p* my limb s a

    che so to   o my he

ad i wish yo   u were he

    re to sap i   t with rum t

        o ease my m

    ind the crew c   all them *bens*

cosa s coi   *sa s* thing s t

    hey live with the e

el s now *op*   *en neer* piet writ

    es to his ans

    up and do   wn *op en ne*

er they ru   n *ik houd van*   u ever at the e

    nd of tim   e go

      ld tun   is they call on *d*

anh the rain se   rpent of ti

    me they call *ai*

        do hwe

    do we d   raw straw s w

ant fo   r died n

    egroes b

        are arsed the

    y f

        all the d

    hows set sa   il from tin

gis with stu   ff and sla

        ves each g

rain in s   and each dro   p in water *or*

    i oh he   al the sk   in of sin

    the sin of s   kin sing

    e the feet o   nly water with sc

        um the s

    hip lies id   le its bones gro

an to b   e with y   ou i

    dle in our e   den sh h hear *de*

    bel a sp   ear in his si

de *mi o*   *bi mi ob*

    i it is but a ru   in of a sto

    ry a rune   to found the f

ind in r   ome to fin

    d the fou   nd in qu   est in their d

ebt ever use   her as you

will they c   all his n

ame fall into t   he blue nig

ht they bra   ve the wa

ter sing a p

raise son   g that is a

frica un

der water a d   aft boy sim

ple in the he   ad he was o

ne grain of s   alt under *t*

ong in my mi   nd gr

ants of l   and to gr

ow cane & g   row ri   ch ruth

can you no   t hear the s

ound of s   and on san   d on b

one water be   ar s the t

ruth i run fro

m a run   e a ru   in of a stor

y to turn o   ver lose find in a   gain she w

ear s but her s   kin what a f

eat this t

ear fate grow s f   at with fe

ar this st   ory can not b

e my only s   on a lad po

our water o   n this s

in aga   inst time

we se   rve them ru

in wring the s   tory dry in

sure feet fus   tic bead   s tendo

ns & ham   string s can   dleslipsearese

yes even go   d and *les an*   *ges* spit *orí o*

ri oh wa   *le* come s h o

me *òrìsà* de

af to their cri

es can we m   end this ma

n this we g   ive them *le m*

ort the sea li

fe water li   ves they as

k for wat   er bread & l

155

ife for *ilé*   *ifè* a fa

                              ir trade i

t was li   ce mice f

            arts and sh   it her fe

                              et flit her

                  e and the   re we use wil

    es & spit   e rose hi

            p tea at the man   se sco

                              nes with j

            am m   ind y our ste

                  p may their s

    ouls rise from t   he har

                  d water   they be

        ing the ro   ot sand ru

                  b s bone c   lean so mu

                                          ch heat

sun s be   ams a story mu

        st bear its we   ight a la

    ss of ten s   he was t

                  oo thin b   y far we bree

                  d then b   ed them i

    f they bo   lt tie t

            hem *ayud*   *ame aide*

                        moi crad

            le it to no   ava   il parse the n

    egro pe   st gna   t open and s

            ift the ti   me sow the ta   res of s

in tears of ne   groes grow g   ibes all rou

            nd eat gr   ub s the ca   ul a ch

                              arm an a

    rk of sou   ls under w   ater we give or

            ders they sta   re *fer*

                              rum th   row *de bon*

es dem my   hope a spi   re to th

        e sky we gi   ve the bon   es order what

            is she but   my story it d   ies in tim

e & within   this tale time d   ies *from tun*

                  is stuff so

                        fine y our eyes w   *ill shine my d*

    ear i have *m*   *es ordres* he trod the grou   nd of tro

y a king in rom   e too he stro

de we hunt fo   wl at the for

t eat sip beer   from gourd s farts

and other sounds   from mouth

and ass boast s

of gold and guineas ten   guinea negroes for

one sapphire for   you rose *j ai*

faim for ruth for t   ruth

ius is just

us   the yams were

bad they sail

on a red tide o   n a die

t of bad y   am and s

our water so   me fish co

me be me   for one day *lève*

lève rise *te*   k mi ju

ju hold it sa   *fe for i* i

t is *ius*   & just *how i m*

iss the ci

ty the s   he negro ent

ices me wit

h her scent traps   my lust my ho   pe for you

can a b   at how about a ra

t the scen

t of you ru   th wafts acros

s oceans *dans ma c*   *hambre le code*

noir my lad

y *noire* how i pet h   er *ifá i*

fa ifá the r   am tie i

t to the ma   st *le san*   g *le sang*

they sang i   sang of grace he   longs for gra

ce were w   e *ewe lu*   *a* or *fon* could

we come be m   e this my bo   d y my *sa*

ng my bon   e a rose bu   sh in the gar

den a sun r   ose in my ede

n *iye i*   *ye iye* the rose is now

sere *dis my ju*   *ju* you no

tek me o   *bi* round go

urds *gate* fo   *ju ju and ob*   *i* they fart p

iss they shi   t in the ed   dy of time *le*

  sang runs we   row out to the ves   sel you ruth

on the qu   ay you smil   e my l

        ust rode her

  then s   he was go   ne was no

    more we des   troy the evi

dence but the   dust end   ures now he

   s got the c   lap *me lua*

you no   *lua* to voy   age thro

  ugh the age *sin*   *deo* without g

od or gold s   in or sap

   phire come be   me it was all

dicta their li   ve s they soap   the negroes rin

   se them lance   their bo   ils

then o   il them the rap

  e of tr   oy ro

   me & af   rica is eve

       r a story a

  s the sun set   s over goré

    e so man   y die they s

  ew the e   yes shut with cat

   gut drag the se   a s for bo

ne for sou   nd for b

    one song &   sound of bon

  e as if   from the de

    ep a son

 g a gro   an we have he

   re ten guinea fowl   for sale ten

guinea hens   we are all *dic*

    ta in g

  od s story   the pea he

    n preens in my e

  den a ra   ce of rud

   e she neg

  roes for be   ads i am

   all *âme* cu

     red in sin what

  reason can we

give so rare n   ever seen on the e

  ve of mu   rder i eat

sup on ha

m & b   read was not a sin

but a mis

take not a mis   take but a s

in they e   at no s   alt to save their

soul s di   d she die a d

our man he   was the cap

tain up and dow   n the deck *wa*

le and *sa*   *de* run from the

field the river t   he raft *ny*

ame me i be   g you bring

the lamp ma

n let s see w   hat we have

here *him d*

ead oh il   *est mort him*   *dead* find

the river run

wale ru   n run *s*

ade run i dif

fer from   the others they di

ffer from o

ther negro   es grin gap   e and ape ci

rce creates the s

tars god the nat

ion circe how   ls des

troys a riot   a circ

us of mur   der she who cre

ates & des   troy s is no mo   re give us this

day our ne   groes our profits   n

yame ny   *ame* we give be

er to *nya*

me mea cul   *pa mea c*

ulpa mea we   b of lies m

y great bla   me and ra

in ran red fort

une flam   es feed s our nig

ht s di

es we stand o   n the rim the cr

ater of   the absolute   *va*   *nona va*

ti revesa do   wn the river we f

led to the fo   rt at the po

rt with the negroe   s w   *ale* and

    sade   flee dow

    n the river   *do not*

read this ruth   *it will destroy you*   s

    am my lad   jot these no

    tes these tunes   *fa la* s

    o fa la m   *i so*   *fa la* i

    t is not a fit j   ob for a la

    d his first ta   ste of s   in once only

    a tas   te of mu

rder leads to a   taste *this is me*

    ant only for y

    our eyes ri   *ma* all is *ri*

    ma gin and be

er gin and bee   r the crew cri

    es yam wa

ter *omi*   they flag n   o wa

    ter yam pap *f*   *o mi omo*

    sade feeds *a*

    de yam p   ap what do

es this me   an *que es es*   *to* they cl

    ap and c   lap and clap

    why th   em not u

s why u   s why no   t them so

    rt the negro   es one by o

    ne all creatio

    n mourn s this a

    ct they are pen

t up for too l   ong *mi have mi o*

    bi in mi tê   *te pot* river ti

    des drag u   s down to the fo

    rt drag the se

    a for bodi   es find the river we

    came from *nyam*   *e* bring the la

mp men my e   yes grow di

    m we le   ave a tra   il a map of s

in for all   who come a   fter the tra

    il leads *wa*   le & *sa*   *de* to the fo

    rt at the port o   n the river *ò*

sun cries   *il doge* o   n his thro

ne the red pop

e too b   less me p

ater for i am s   in what the ca   use loud ran

g the sin   g and so

ng of sang

le sang le   song *le s*

on el s   *on* there was a   gue so

me fa   int piss & bi

le there was   but me

n must eat a   h but the p

us the pi   ss & the b

ile sad *sad*   *e* sad sa

d *sade* o   ne deal

led to an o   ther and ano

ther the she   negroes sin

g sa

d songs sing   song voi

ces at da   wn we beg

in they l

imp they cry *act*   *six scene*

ten daw   n *wars with nig*

ht cir

ce sage   *and oracle i*

s centre stag   *e with her wa*

nd she sen   *ds storms to be*

at us all   *about* where e

ver the winds   throw u

s there we plan   t a flag for nat

ion po   pe or kin

g strum me a   tune at dawn be

fore i di   e she   rent my re

d cape su   ch a grand gard   en with stag

s grouse and   deer an e   den the lad la

y dead and a   nother & anot

her they a   ll lay d

ead *i hate the s*   *in ruth so*

why d   *o i* sif

t the ne

groes one   from the o

ther & stru

m me a tun   e louts all w

ho lust for a sl   ut not i pra

y for me ru   th *o*

ra or   *a or*   *a* pray i s

ay at da   wn it be

gins i sal

ute *il doge*   the king in u

s in *ius*

pin hi   m down her

too we ho   ne the rag

e of the age

wed the wo   e in we to *i*

us yam n

egroes we b   e we be f

ree now they fa   ll we cag   e them was i

t necessity hit   her hard we three

and her pa   ps the dog

and her p   ups play me

ewe him   *lua* she *e*

do we had su   ch a time rut

h the corn wa   s rip

e in the fields

as were you mea   sure the law with c

are not too mu   ch jus

ice with a to

w & a row &   a row row ro

w we fal

l our lies t   ake wing so

ar to jo   in our ame

ns & *aves* how   did we get he

re just u

s ruth you and m   e in the g

arden our ed   en will he

throw u   s out as he

has be   fore in that i

n stance of s   in i see all

they we   d woe to w   ant to wa

r to water   hey ho

ld her un   der a cloud

of nec   essity and rain   we sa

iled so man   y man neg

roes she ne   groes yam   negroes hi

t her if she res   ists i mis   s the city

ruth y   our li   ps it grow s d

rear and sad   and we are b

ut slav   es to sin   our pi

g got go   t our pig   in a po

t the di   n of negroes

the lu   re of wa

ter and   the lu

st for war fins   find the fu

n in frenzy in s

cent of *le*   *sang* in n

egro me   at in go   re *tear this*

up des   *troy this a*

fter you re   *ad it do not*

read it i di

d not writ

e it it i   *s it is*   *not* not a stor

y or a tal   e to be tol   d our ne

gro our p   ig in a po   t we mis

took negr   oes for s

laves sla   ves for ne

groes i rid   e my mar

es of night   hard alm

s for the   poet of t   roy we

beg *new scene*   *il doge sno*

res a vase of as   *ter s and rose*

s near

by my soul

flag s some di

ve others a

re throw   n others th

row thems

elves *een hand*   *uma perna la*

main el ma   *no el pie u*   *n bras a*

fist an   arm a   leg a

hand a h   ead a co

ld tear ta   me this she

negro ta   ke her   arm the ro

pe men ro   me shin

es so do   es troy in the nig   ht of my mi

nd cast th   em o   ver a cas

e of port win   e for y

ou my ma   n *it was a c*   *ase of m*

urder i te   *ll you* in th

at insta   nce of s   in he sees al

l i tire can s   it no mo

re cl   ams feed on we

eds weeds fe   ed on fle

sh we din   e on neg

ro me   at grow fa

t the son   g calms *fa so*   *la fa s*

o la mi m   *i fa so*   *la* am ra

m am s   am i a   m am *âm*

e am ha   m h   am w

e am h   am a   m h

am *you we*   re *so wa*   *n the day i to*

ld you my sh   *ip was ah*   *out to sa*

il dum d   um de du   m we bro

ught them to mark   et fat she

negroes

a bust   of our ma

d king near my b   ed i ti

re gr   ow sad *sa*

me scene ag   *ain il doge ga*

pes & grin   *s a rict*

us will we me

et aga   in at the sto

ne cairn with the mo   ss grip her fa   st we fast be

fore mu   rder shun the li

ght *will you sh*   *un me r*   *uth as the t*

ruth of my wo   *rds finds y*

ou i   ron for *òg*   *ún* water for *ò*

sun sang for s   *ango* i seek the sk

i   n in   kin they   the k

in in sk   in we rend

er them in   to n

egroes into b

one s   and & wat

er su   ch wit he

had the ne   gro the wo

ods we hid   e & li   e on m

oss *wal*   e sade & a   *de* hide i

n the woo   ds no res

pite fro   m o   ver with her o

ver with hi   m they se

t traps fo   r *wa*   *le sad*

e & a   *de* i serve h

im they se   rve me sit

rapt at my wo   rds such an   ger pent up fo

r so lo   ng to re

st and rep   air my so

ul i d   raw near t

o thee g   od pra

y the saint s he

ar my p   lea s such a fe   at from k

in to s   kin we tra

verse the se   as let us in

vest in ne   groes a bull ma   rket bring b

ell brin   g drum & tars

bring *do*   *n don* & *go*   *n gon* the op

era over we d   rop her o

ver we eat e   gg drop so

up fish ro   e & h

am *scene nev*   *er seen be*

fore the wo   ods drab and d

rear in win   ter the negro

es hew woo   d for fire *wale*

sade & *ad*   *e* are prey su

ch anger i ha   ve never see

n the la   d lay dead no mo

re his age we

are lat   e they are so

late for ti   me we sal

ute you my cap   tain my lie   ge lord they r

an and ra

n too la   te for *w*

le for *s*   *ade* & *ade* par   se the t

ruth in m   urder in s

in we are t   heir bane ene   mies to their lif

e and we a   re of f to me

et our fat   e their fa

te a date i da   re not mi

ss foo   d for fi

sh for eel fea   ring the truth t   hey fret an

d fret we eat   ham and spu

ds with port

we rou   se the su

n with our a   cts they with t

heir cries the po   et writes in sa

nd a pra   ise song for t

roy & r   ome for f

ez & for the cit   y for gold tin

gis for all pla   ces at the e   nd of t

ime & out of ti   me for *a*

fer the *ter*

ra afra for y   ou & all that i

s lost first we   bream the shi

p of sea we   eds be fo   re we set sa

il they pee   r into ti

me drug of a   ll who li   ve on bo

ard there were d   rum s & b

ells so all co   uld dan

ce at eden the   re is bre

am & carp in ou   r pond they fi

sh for do   ry up the run

gs to the to   p of the ma

st lad wha   t do you s   ee *mi*

se en sce   *ne il doge we*

ars a red tog   *a the goat ru*   *ns* so we can li

ve in ease so   you can li

ve in great e   ase figs and or   ange s hot bu

ns tea a se   cret ra   ce so a

lien to all we   hold dear *the*

n she shows u

s her bare a   *rse and fall*

t at night ba   t s come out t

o play how ju   st is this on

e bag of sp   uds with grub

s the gib   es the cur   se s they cu

    rse us in t   heir own words

        the most fou

l words *in*   *da gora ri*

    ze mate ma   *te* who cur

se d me what   is this c   urse that i sho

    uld be so lo   st even the ora   cle cur

se s u   s leave s us   to our fat

    es at ves   pers we rec   ite god ver

se s most fo   ul words wha

    t do we cre   ate he b   et her

    at card s he lo   st her drat

that rat my   suit was   heart s him

    up there gold

    nails in his h   ands fe

et on his he   ad gold tho

    rns save the s   lave in u

s in y   ou when the g   ong so

    unds s run in bet   ween our am

    en s & our *a*   *ve* mari as run i sa

y from our me   as & culp

    a s run for y o   ur life run *wa*

le run ru   n *sade* r   un run *ad*

    e run *w*   *ale* and *sa*

de run fo   r their liv   e s *sade* ha

    s sore tea   ts *scene il do*   ge a red tog

a a man   *e of gold h*   *air he fum*

    es the negro i   s a pest to b   e rid of him

    up there nai   led to woo

d to the mas   t we slid   e on a tide of pro

    fit to murde   r rob them o

f all they cr   eate she spins a t   op drops

    a ston   e into the de   ep be co

    me s bone *te*   *amo te am*

o on   *ly you r*   *uth but now s*

    he has my mi   *nd in de*

    ath he deals t   he cards we si

t rapt who w   ill win her the fi

    re is hot   get the to

ng s & the iro   n s she i

s his now

the sun go   es round as eve

r how lo   ng had they la   in there sk

in on fi   re rub the s

kin with o   il *wal*

e and *sade* ha   ve one go   at *agbo*

the ob   *a* sobs ag

ain & a   gain the *oba* so

bs *oh ye ye*   *lantic oh*   *oh ye ye oh*

omi omi omi oh   we be aro   oun *ẹbọra*   *omi oh*

omi oh   omi *ojú*   *ye ye lantic oh*   *omi omi omi oh*

ẹyọ   aro orun   oh ye ye oh ye ye oh

lantic oh   ca ri be eh oh   oh omi ero

oh ye ye oh   ma abo oh   oh mi *ẹbọra*

ye ye lan   tic oh ca ri be   eh sho ala o mi o

o dò   o fa un   sho ca ri be   eh sho omi nla

lan tic oh   oh ye ye oh   oh ab wa ma

e oh ye ye oh   omi o omi *ọmú*   abo wa ba

oh ye ye oh   ma abu oh   ise ni ise ini   omi ara

abu di ni   omi ok un   oh oh ye ye oh

omi omi   oh omi mí mó   a la o fa un   ma abu oh

oh ye ye   gari be eh   oh ye ye oh mi

sho soh a bwa   o mi abo wa ba

oh ye ye oh   oh lan tic oh   omi tú tù

oh ye ye omi ara   orun omi òsun   oh ye ye o

omi dí dùn oh   omi e lu   ju oh omi   òsà

o   ye ye we b   e se   a kin wa

wa   water ki   n be cam

from omi   *ìyè we be*   *ẹbọra àkì*   ash

es and sa   lt for the bo   die s   of kin un

der the sk   in of s   ea whe

re repo

se the bo   ne sou   ls of kin

can y   ou not he

ar *sub voce*   the voi   ces *au*

di of kin *a*   *udi* in the wind   part wat

er part bo   ne par

t salt *le*   sel la sa

l *salis* in *le*

sang sa   lt in the e   ye salt i

          n the h   air salt un   der the na

                    ils sal   t in the e

  ars sa   lt in the no   se salt on the s

                    kin salt un   der the sk

          in of the s   ea bo   ne sal

                    t sk   im the sk   in of the se

                    a for the wo   rds the voic

  es of k   in the trap   of rea

                    son binds u   s in the net

          of time we s

kim the scu   m of prof

                    its they their k

          in long lo   ng ago th

                    ere wa   s a tal

e to b   e told a to   ugh ma

          n rough on a   ll the she

                    negroes too stern   men of ste

  rn mi   en we ar

          e we run our li   ves by b

ell & go   ng the ring s o

                    f sin gro   w ever wid

  e the terns ma   ke rings abo   ve so to

                    o the fi   ns in the se

  a we ea   t ham we e   at bre

          ad we eat fi   sh fresh fro

                    m the deep   *w*

ale and *sa*   *de* e   at fr

          esh fish f   rom the r

                    iver we b   e fresh wa

  ter neg   roes the sea is *ma*

          i is *mère* i   s *mer* is

mar *ema*   & *mater* i

          s *madre* is   ma is   *omi ò*

                    ab wa ma   *e* gar

den grubs al   l over me a   m hot the he

          at we are de   af to their cri

  es *ba le*   g *ba* l   *eg ba*

          leg b   *a leg   ba*

leg   *ba leg* give th

em the se

a to pro   ve to kin

g nation & f   lag lend your e

ar to their cri   es mine

too they giv   e them   selves li

fe we gi   ve them the li   fe of bone n

ow the sea gi   ves up the se

cret of bo   ne es oh

es es oh   es *os o*   s they ask fo

r water we g   ive them s

ea they as   k for bread we

give them se

a they ask for lif   e we give them o

nly the sea *was*   *that a fair*

trade ruth i   *ask you i*

am a fair   *man* by b   ell and go

ng the crew   dance a re

el on board the   negroes play the d

rums to the de

ep s with them   they sin

g as they fa   ll bles   s me *pater*

i am all   sin by wo

rd and d   eed bless him *pa*

ter give him this d   ay his b

read his wat   er his profit s a

bove blue oce   an of sky

waits cal   m no clo

ud under us bl   ue sea the ear

th groans it w   as the dri

ve for pro   fit *douce do*

uce mi amo   *r we be i*

bo we be sho   *na ban*   *tu we b*

e fa   *nte edo & ra*

da that da   *y at the man*

se we at   *e were sa*

ted with ve

al and wine bet   *ween us there we*

re no wil   *es did I du*   *pe you ther* e was on *ly ought* we ga ve them go

d & gave the m good they gi

ve us good & & go d be

ar the we ight of ours

ins light as the su n s beams there i

s shit & pi ss bile & pu

s there is s in he rose will

i will he hew a beam of wo

od for the mas t strong to ha

ng them from

did I write t hat ham and fi

sh roe dates and fi gs sweet me

at s we din e on neg

ro meat & o ranges a lass of t

en serve s u

s mind y our s tep now lad

on bread and w ater we bree

d them ble ss me *pat*

er for i have set a snare for *wa* *le & sad*

e a trap for h

is feet a sna

re for hers *w* *ale* and *sade* are ti

red we grow tir ed more mis

fortunes than i can no

ink my pen ca n write no mo

re here on the s

kin of the sea

how do i ge

t this to y ou if only i c

ould write on wa

ter my sins ha

ve the s ea say to yo

u what i can

not i he ar only the ro

ar of r

aw water t he sea s voi

ce a fis t to the he ad if you hap

pen upon my s in the sea gi

ves up it s d read secret w

ho can bear t   o hear the bo

nes of g   od lie here

scene he sin   *gs* a pint of a   le & on

e dead ne   gro on the alt

ar of our gre   ed where li

ve our *la*   res and *pena*   *tes* we ab

use the ab

solute in g   od goo

d & ma

n   for a t   roy ou

nce of go   ld a ba

r of s   alt we be   at our h

eads *oh ye ye*

oh ti   me is tard   y late in tim

e i lon   g for cold lak

es the harsh wind   s of the dow

ns the bli   ss of the p   ast my hope

traps me m   y na

me is you *y*   *ou big man*

me i see yo   *u to wri*

te wri   *te a*

ll ti

me me wa   *le you wr*   *ite for m*

e such an un   common man *me i s*

ay you writ   e on pap   *er i wri*

te *de*   *ar sade you h*

e my queen e   *ver me i mi*   *ss you and a*

de al   *l my lif*   *e i a*

m do   ne he ta   ke s the pa

per e   ats it the   n he fa

ll s on his li   ps *sa*

de fé   *mi i*

fá if   *á if*   *á* if o

nly *ifá* he fa   lls to the we

ight & wa   it in w

ater i ca   ll his na

me & f

all too t   o my on

ce my no   nce queen of the ni
            ger the sa   ble o
    ne *nig*   ra afra
        sa   d
                e oh ye ye afr   i
        ca oh o
                ver and o
    ver the *o*   ba   s
                        o
            b
                                        s

Behtemba Agbehe Gholahan Fasuyi Abifarin Olurun
Fadairo Abiona Nuru Ohunade Dolap Moyo
Olufunke Olupitan Falana Esi
Kobena Atoapem Kwesi
Wahe Sade
Ade

Ébora

seas   there is o

                    this tithmurder my lord   oh oh

oracle   within   over   my liege lord

                        my fortyurless   time within loss

                    there are   my us

            oh oh   a sin   *ora*   my we

                            ora   ashes   *video*   my fate

            my god   *ora*   over   *video*

                            ora pro   *ifa*   *video*

                                        ifa under crew from

am   captain *ifa i*

        ftord   this is but an oration   of loss   own from

fa   time sands the losswithsay   slave

        fa rose for Ruth   falkding from

                    and   i am   writer

                        over   for truth   from

                visions   &   mortality

over and over   over   suppose truth

            the crewtothinga sobs   then

        no provisionsfinding a way   there is fate

                le p'tit mort   found   there is creed

from is   scent of mortality   there is

            to was   a rule   oh oh

        ought evidence   she   water parts

                        falls   the *oba* sobs again

fa fa fa   suppose   the other seas

            falhing   *ifa ifa ifa i* with she

truth   a rose   to   negroes

there is creed   the   port   man

there is seven   over   negroes

                              salve the slave
           this is but an oracle *salve* to sin   sihe *oba* sobs
   video subliminal fields the loss within   i am
                          am   and *ave*
there is creed   lord *ve*   *visions*   ave
there and *ave* er   a rose i say
        a rose for Ruth *here is* the *oba* sobs
             no provision *and*   oh oh
             oracle   for truth
from is   suppose truth
        to was   there are   *then* the seas
finding as *save* the yam oh oh   with she
                   found   cut right *ghost*
              and *save* the yam ox *port*
                         negroes   not th *if the* at murder my lord
payment you *say* liege lord ought evidence   suppose *ifa*
             then   what for   my dei *fa i*
    fa   my us
fae rat   the rat   truth   my we   a rose
my god fa the cat   over   falling   my fate
the cat got the rat   & sunder crew from
        over   with *captain*
           own fresh *she* falls   &
found the crime   slave   over
         a rose *the crew* touching   under from
be absolute   writer   found africa there is fate
        underfrom   there is creed
            water   mo *cut the* ear   there is proved
     justice   dange *rous*   oh oh
do you hear *that the* law
        le mort   sound to *raise* the *oba* sobs again
        le p'tit mort   *she dead*   sos sos sos   *ifa ifa ifa i*
                  the died   os
             scent of mortality   *os*   the
     seven   I hear *a le be* le/s
seas   she *us os*   ring out
Dear Ruth   this th *ills*   save us *os*
    ifai fafa   salve & save
this is a tale   falling   to our souls   time within loss
told cold   t *part* & turn
a yarn a *story* ones   *ora*   over
        &   & *ora*
             over *the inner* suthls
do I   my fortunes *ora pro*   us souls
have   bone souls   water parts

                              dear Lisa
                    Dave ask/s that i
when did we decide you   Circe the crone   these words come from his lips
thought one hag seer   my hand shapes them   she
                              the sibrestidying   sh/h
              apes all lips   of dead
    sing sing earp   of died   not so loud
                    they sang   sing sat time
    didn't the bell ring   a sad tune   oh oh
I come from the north   le song with more notes   el song   my ass
              the dales again   no i can
land of mist   like   ann   my goat bag
of hoar-frost   ann   ann   palm will be
              the time and ship of sin   heaven
    sow the seven seas   groan too   &&
        froo with ave/s   the plan in   the din   the
    with ash din   of dying   why did we   writ in
        decide when did we the dead   decide   sand
              the died   the dead   live rent   sing i say
    i come from   my own   my   lives
i come from   the north   very own the
    the north   dales the   land   hey hey ho
        dales of mist land   of hoar frost
        there is rust in   the time and date of hoar frost
              of sin insure the time and date
    he had an ace   of sin
                    i a sequence of
        queens   one
        king   chu
        Sam   the rum
                    dear Ruth can a tale be
    mortality by the tail   ever
    mortality why the tail   if told
    on the sun   cold   a secret race
    mazina   *underwriters
    mai   calms   lives   of writ/s &   rent/s
        calms
        calms   the truth
        calms   to the right   to be sure
                    this is but
    writ in sand   an oration
    write in sand   a tale
    lives life   old
    rent life   as sin   is new
    when did we decide

the seas
there is   with she
creed there is   fate the negroes
is oh   man   there is   negros oracle
creed there lord   there are   fate there
my lie oh lord   oh oh   oh oracle
ashes there are   my *deus*
olmohus   over
my we   ashes   *ifa*   my fate
my god   *ifa*   over
sunder crew from   *ifa i*
ifa captain   *ifa i*
fa
fa   own from   *ifa i*
fa fa   slave   falling
fa   over   under from
fa   writer   fall   &
ing from   over
the crew   mortality   touching there   &
is fate   overt   water parts
the crew   there   the *oba* touching there creed
is fat *de mort*   there
le p'tis mo here   oh   is creedh
there   the seas sobs mortality
is   oh   oh the *ifa ifa i*
sobs   she   again   the
seven   falls   *ifa ifa ifa i*
seas *ifaifaifa*   over   the   *ora*
seven   falling time   *ora*   to
within   seas   port   *ora*
ora   *ora pro* over   time
this time within   *ora*
this is but an   over   within   *ora* oration
my fortunes   time sands the loss
with a sin   you say time   in i am
video video video   this is lord   but an o
who says ration of loss   time
sands   i say visions   the loss   a rose
a rose for Ruth with   over and over   in i am
and lord of   the *oba* sobs
no provisions   for loss this from is   o
ver and o   to was   suppose truth   ver
the seas   then   the *o*   water parts
finding a way   *ba* so   with she   the *oba* sobs no pro
found   visions from is   negroes
to was   man   a port sow

179

                    dear Lisa
        Dave ask/s
                    that i   to the right   write Clara
    to be sure   the words   the tune
        to you
            this is come from his lips   tears   but my hand shapes the air
    them   an oration   &   it calms me   sh/h
                a tale   apes all   but then the drum/s
        sing   old   & oh the drum/s
all night   why are we here   as   not so loud   sing
            they sing   didn't
they pray for death the bell ring new   where are
not le p'tit mort   le sang   oh oh
        they shout lisalet the crone   dance   el song
we act the next but last line on   lisa dance
    my ass
    the facts   a/gape hot   dance sing again   what does it mean
                sings
            Dear Ruth captain pain   my gold bag of
        can a tale   palm wine   sad tune   it is
            they lie
be told   they lie   they
        sow the seven seas   notes   they groan   ma ma
Dear Ruth   with ave/s   the sun moi je am   mai
    with ash if a tale a fortune in forts he sing am   she
        daughter pint of gin and he told and   him oba am
                    sing i say the   this is an oration heaves
ora   my   own   to   him ask wien am   my   & for me
ora   they/ov sobs again fro   groans   the din   of
ora   the candle flames ho drinking he/s   writ in
    the tale is old   when did we decide   once the   dead   the
        old as sin   there is ruse   indied   sand
        i come   from   insure   sconce lives rent life
Circe   he had an   the north   the   dies
    the crone   dale a sequence land
    the hag   of mist   of hoar frost
    the seer   queens   one   the time
        she of the stars   date   chu
her lips gape   Sam the rum   of sin
wind strum/s the air sings a tune there is   us   dear Ruth   &
a sad tune
he strum/s the oud can a tale be   os
with no notes   the ship cradled told   there is bone
why does the light none shine so   moi
        our lust   a secret race   moi
        our loss   piss   it rains
        all that is old lives   & of writ/s underwriters
& rent/s   in this new age   bile cede   he am
                    the truth   ran pus   am

told

ba/ba cold sh/h

iya the have your

ifa clarion ear i slave me

osudays rave i *reve* now for *je* do you

me A clear brain oasis it hear a detail him

reves the no mist in the vale port and an pass

les the dray cart *reves* in the He was peas

the bay in the cart pleas of

of niah rolip clop up gaclop hard slap

& den you and her and i Ruth will slap

the slave stag/s sobs oh boar/s &

sail the sobs Sam deer carp ush & mud huts vfirst

only mate the the river doves when

we will rush the huts there *nóu* if

will be dogs sobs & fish ashes let we rush de &ap/n

to seal grouse *omi se* this owls & craot

tit/s opea/ben/s too a/wr skin hud over pigs and of over

hold him negroes & she again sin this

negroes *je* lead bred of of *reve* hát greed

a deal *reve* pain has my

elation ali asei tm *mes* new ran t seeds the

erase this riot that hat my the seal

on erase me sea/s drase tim an man deal feeds the

ave well lust done for

ave i see you tin the Kate a sin for gold

ave comes clad we will rest

slave in in fur rest ush the captain

ring save the *ave/s* rest howny the pet many

cara save the *salve/s* my she

negro how do the *vale/s* too you ask me I beg dem fo *Ayo*

fut Smote the slaves forty we parse i

fsayi omo Ben the lad the deed is lay dead it one *mi* *omo*

fo mi pic/kin or *mi* bi geowateawith

bite him dabe sun's rays told we

him big codd an hot praise old the

him *fun/fun* dead the gibde it one

note a is held him lesbher a an job well

thlynbgro aria done for the Clair

hey djtain Kate for falasatyt the

hey & pain th Ruth &rat a tat for

pain *le pain le* *pain* etc pan pant here's ara banta tat

pans ed the paint row row

Dan Jon & s Will & it s lhe arde the roar i

the areevof ates watery tale

found   a   gin my us   in afric?
y/our ear   a   rum   my   negroes
they go   re aster/s oh oh   our mig   cam fo m found africa   the mast must be teak men
        the deed under who can cure me   s
ocaics &   wat captain ver   for yo the cur   that that   proved
      justi   thw   from   dangero   for je ifa that hat
the   the how my lie g   lord   deep   pour ri cut the cards
      days   par   nf   ig   & der from ifa i   I won the throw
we ks   my plea is negli   field/ser   sos s   fa   luce
fa   my fa e   from us   i say   of   sle y doge
comes fa   for os mort   ra   aces   she smiles
cut her open in li ll be   & justice   star   be   b smile
    the noise rth   co   the   I   in lives & am   a dischf   le
it i   rt as th   is   ove m   save   ing   throw f   ing
      le p'tit m he   crew   ig   en   sky   Ruth   throw them
              of   t of mortality   in rations murder s   is fate crusts
but why R   the no   sum   am   tone & f   e   e see there is creed
      th   ones   she do the stars   ap   i   nig   if shine there is der   if only
              & fi   s   in mur   mi de us   & y   w   y ide   oh oh
her sha   faifaifa   salve our souls   fo   again
    with   nt an   ge   if only ifa   nag   trust   se   ifa ifa ifa i
serve   round b   uda   is all wrong port   the the oba sobs again
and fi   men   rum ra ight   ov ere was piss cum
seas   more rum   &   g   Ruth
fer   tho   ms   o a   salve the slave   they sang &
    with   m and and   my   des   sang w   se with sin we map
      uncomm   into salve   ora pro you   y   later water/s leak   time
      vid   leo   withine a sea   f   ng   pu   b   th
  me   this is   t over a   ound   ti   days sang   av cord   such
    the   pi   her i say groa   ve   a rose i pen   t   y   der   further
  j   the rose for Ruth fat nig dugs here   er tea   e   the er seery   t
  th t go   you there ard   lo   n ation all lord   payment
n God no we wer write   for tr   to   yo   uace cap for my what for
y   Gods hear m   c   th   of li   on li   pose tru the negroes with
            toys ov   ch   do you hear the lute
f   ing lady gold   fo uld cut the cord of this story sound to r   oba sobs
take every thing   is   en   on   fro   est my case
cum grano   n   a so   out is   sow   in negligence
with a grain of salt dire vision at ve   ar   tell /s my p   l   nights water parts
        the be   ing   ought evi   the t   on   b   necessity
   R reed   then   vedic   mu   negr s   ave t you
th   a   nst su nth   a rose pro   you   to ile ife
told cold   a   i   s groes   sow the sea   n   r my lord
h   my lie   lord um   sm   nding
him hi   with sos   de   ey Ruth   os   w   s de s &
h   too us   I m she fa   atio   Ben   reason

Glossary

WORDS AND PHRASES OVERHEARD ON BOARD THE *ZONG*

Arabic

rotl: unit of weight or
measurement

Dutch

bel: bell
bens: thing
geld is op: money is spent
hand: hand
ik houd van u: I love you
op en neer: up and down
tak: arm
tong: tongue

Fon

Age: water god
Da: snake god that coils
around the universe and
supports the earth
Lisa: female deity connected
with the moon
Mawu: male deity connected
with the sun

French

aide moi: help me
aile: wing
âme: soul
ange: angel
coeur: heart
eau: water
il est mort: he is dead
j'ai faim: I'm hungry
j'ai soif: I'm thirsty
je: I
laver: to wash
main: hand
mer: sea

mort: death
mot juste: the just word
père: father
pied: foot
pour moi: for me
rêve: dream
rêver: to dream
sang: blood
santé: health
tais toi: be quiet

Greek

beta: second letter of Greek
alphabet

Hebrew

aleph: first letter of
alphabet

Italian

il doge: the duke

Latin

afer: African (male)
afra: African (female)
audi: hear or listen
ave: hello, good-bye
culpa: fault
cum grano salis: with a grain
of salt
deo: god
deus: god
dicta: a saying; in law, com-
ments that are pertinent to
a case but do not have
direct bearing on the out-
come.
ego: I

esse: to be
ferrum: iron
inter pares: among equals
lares and penates: household
gods
mea: my
niger: black (male)
nigra: black (female)
os: bone
pater: father
ratio: reason; in law, the
short for *ratio decidendi*, the
central reason for a legal
decision
sal: salt
salve: hello, good-bye
sin: without
sum: I am
te deum: early Christian
hymn of praise
ventus: wind
video: I see

Portuguese

belo: beautiful
coisa: thing
lindo: beautiful
perna: a leg

Spanish

ayudame: help me
cosa: thing
mano: hand
para mi: for me
pie: foot
que es esto: what is this
son: the song
yo: I

Shona

afa: he/she has died
ari: he/she is
asi: but
ave: so that he/she can be
bere: hyena
bete: cockroach
bodo: no
dare: court
dede: baboon
derere: okra
dura: granary
duri: mortar
ega: alone
enda: go
fini: cruelty
gano: axe for fighting
gate: clay pot
go: wasp
godo: jealous
gora: baby without father; vulture
gore: year
gudo: baboon
gura: cut
guti: when it's cloudy and about to rain, overcast
inda: louse; go
indiani: who are you?
ini: me/I
ipa: give
isa: put into
ishe: god, king, creator, queen
ita: do
iva: become
mai: mother
mari: money
mate: spit
na: with/by/and
ndega: on my own
ndini: it's me
nego: by a wasp
nemari: with money
oda: she wants
oga: by him/herself

pera: finished
redu: ours
rema: fool
revesa: speak the truth
rima: darkness
riva: trap
rize: scorpion
rudo: love
rume: big man
sa: like
sema: revulse
seva: gossip
sora: grass
sure: behind
taita: sister
tese: together
tiki: amount of money
toga: on our own
tora: take
ura: womb, intestines
uri: you are
vanoa: they have seen
vati: they said
vene: owners
vese: all of them
viga: hide

Twi

cedis: unit of currency in Ghana
Nyame: name of God

West African Patois

lava lava: talk
tiki tiki: money

Yoruba

ague: fast
àse: may it manifest
aso won: their clothes
ba ba: father
ebo: sacrifice
ebora: underwater spirits
ebo orí: sacrificial food for Orí
Efun: Yoruba deity

Èsù: Yoruba deity
fun fun: white
gbo mi mu: drink water
Ifà: divination
Ilé Ifè: capital city of Yorùbáland in Nigeria
ilé wa: our house
Inle: divine physician who is also a fisherman and hunter
ìyá: mother
ìyà: suffering, tribulation
iye: mother
ju ju: an item which is believed to have protective qualities
ní mi ni ran: remind me
ní ran: remember
oba: king, ruler
ode: hunter
ó d àbò: until my/your return
ó d ola: until tomorrow
odù: statements from oracle
Ògún: Yoruba deity of iron
Olú: God
olú femi: god loves me
olú sèyí: god did this
omi: water
omi dídùn: sweet water
omi ebora: water in which spirits reside
omi mímó: holy or life-giving water
omi òkun: ocean water
omi osa: water from the lagoon
omi se oore: water did a kind thing
omi tútù: cool water
omo: child, offspring
omo è: her child
omo e: your child
orí: head
Òsun: river goddess
owó: money
owó mi: my money
wa àgbò: look for the ram

Manifest

AFRICAN GROUPS & LANGUAGES

Bantu
Edo
Ewe
Fante
Fon
Ibo
Lua
Rada
San
Shona
Twi

ANIMALS

ant
asp
ass
bat
bee
boar
bream
carp
cat
clam
cod
deer
dog
dory
dove
eel
fish
fowl
grouse
hare
hen
hog
lion
mare
nits
owl
pig
pup
rat
raven
sole
sow
stag
tit mouse
toad
wolf

BODY PARTS

arm
bras
cunt
ear
eye
feet
finger
fist
hand
head
heel
hip
leg
lips
mano
nail
nose
ongle
paps
perna
pied
tak
teat
tit
toe
tong
torso

CREW

Alf
Dan
Dave
Don
Ed
Hamz
Hans
Jesus
Jim
Jon
Mike
Ned
Peter
Piet
Roy
Sam
Ted
Tim
Tom

FOOD & DRINK	NATURE	WOMEN WHO WAIT
ale	asters	Ama
beer	bog	Ans
bread	cairn	Clara
carp	corn	Clair
cider	dale	Eva
cod	fen	Eve
corn	field	Grace
dates	garden	Mary
éclairs	glen	Miss Circe
egg	hay	Rosa
gin	mist	Rose
ham	moss	Ruth
herb	ocean	Sue
hops	peat	Tara
jam	rose	Um
kale	sea	
meat	sky	
oranges	stone	
pea	stook	
pear	sun	
pie	tares	
port	vale	
rice	yew	
roe		
rose water		
rum		
scone		
sion (water parsley)		
soup (egg drop)		
spud		
tea		
veal		
water		
whey		
wine		

Notanda

There is no telling this story; it must be told

In 1781 a fully provisioned ship, the *Zong*,[1] captained by one Luke Collingwood, leaves the West Coast[2] of Africa with a cargo of 470 slaves and sets sail for Jamaica. As is the custom, the cargo is fully insured. Instead of the customary six to nine weeks, this fateful trip will take some four months on account of navigational errors on the part of the captain. Some of the *Zong*'s cargo is lost through illness and lack of water; many others, by order of the captain are destroyed: "Sixty negroes died for want of water . . . and forty others . . . through thirst and frenzy . . . threw themselves into the sea and were drowned; and the master and mariners . . . were obliged to throw overboard 150 other negroes."[3]

Captain Luke Collingwood is of the belief that if the African slaves on board die a natural death, the owners of the ship will have to bear the cost, but if they were "thrown alive into the sea, it would be the loss of the underwriters."[4] In other words, the massacre of the African slaves would prove to be more financially advantageous to the owners of the ship and its cargo than if the slaves were allowed to die of "natural causes."

Upon the ship's return to Liverpool, the ship's owners, the Messrs Gregson, make a claim under maritime insurance law for the destroyed cargo, which the insurers, the Messrs Gilbert, refuse to pay. The ship's owners begin legal action against their insurers to recover their loss. A jury finds the insurers liable and orders them to compensate the ship's owners for their losses—their murdered slaves. The insurers, in turn, appeal the jury's decision to the Court of King's Bench, where Lord Mansfield, the Lord Chief Justice of England presides, as he would over many of the most significant cases related to slavery.[5] The three justices, Willes, Buller, and Mansfield, agree that a new trial should be held. The report of that decision, *Gregson v. Gilbert*, the formal name of the case more colloquially known as the *Zong* case, is the text I rely on to create the poems of *Zong!* To not tell the story that must be told.

"The most grotesquely bizarre of all slave cases heard in an English court," is how James Walvin, author of Black Ivory, describes the *Zong* case.[6] In the long struggle in England to end the transatlantic slave trade and, eventually, slavery, the *Zong* case would prove seminal: "The line of dissent from the *Zong* case to the successful campaign for abolition of slavery was direct and unbroken, however protracted and uneven."[7] I have found no evidence that a new trial was ever held as ordered, or whether the Messrs Gregson ever received payment for their murdered slaves, and, before the first trial had begun, the good Captain Collingwood who had strived so hard to save the ship's owners money had long since died.

It is June—June 15, 2002 to be exact, a green and wet June in Vermont. I need—I must, I decide—keep a journal on the writing of *Zong!* I have made notes all along but there is a shift: "Am going to record my thoughts and feelings about this journey," I write, "as much a journey as the one Captain Collingwood made; like him I feel time yapping at my heels—have but 3 months to deliver this ms."[8] I flirt with the idea of immersing myself in as much information as I can find about this incident involving the slave ship *Zong*. I begin reading a novel about it, but am uncomfortable: "A novel requires too much telling," I write, "and this story must be told by not telling—there is a mystery here—the mystery of evil (*mysterium iniquitatis* to quote Ivan Illich)."[9] Should I keep on reading? "If what I am to do is find their stories in the report – am I not subverting that aim by reading about the event?"

I have brought two legal texts with me to Vermont, one on contracts, the other on insurance law—a branch of contract law. The boredom that comes with reading case after case is familiar and, strangely, refreshing, a diversion from going somewhere I do not wish to go. I find out what I knew before: that essentially a contract of insurance or indemnity provides that a sum of money will be paid when an event occurs which is adverse to the interests of the person who has secured insurance. But I am hunting for something—anything—to give me some bearing, since I am, metaphorically speaking, at sea, having cut myself off from the comfort and predictability of my own language—my own meaning. A sentence catches my eye: "Surely, little in the way of authority is required to support the statement of Lord Sumner in *Gaunt* that there is no 'loss' when the insured brings about the insured event by his own act."[10] Since Captain Collingwood deliberately drowned the Africans on board his ship, I reason, he cannot, therefore, claim a loss. Does this make me feel better? About the law? But a jury of his peers found otherwise; further, how can there not be a "loss" when 150 people are deliberately drowned? Collingwood was not a seasoned captain: Prior to this fateful voyage his involvement in the slave trade had been as a ship's surgeon. In this capacity, however, he would have known that maritime law in England at that time exempted insurance claims for the natural death of slaves (which itself begs the question whether the death of someone who is a slave can ever be "natural"), but held, and ominously so, that insurers were liable when slaves were killed or thrown overboard as a result of rebellions, revolts, or uprisings.

Like Captain Collingwood, I am now fully launched on a journey. Unlike the good captain, however, I do not feel fully provisioned, indeed, uncertainty is my familiar. Can I really fashion poems from this modest report of a legal case, *Gregson v. Gilbert*? About a story about which there is no telling?

Another green and misty morning in Vermont—I sit on a porch, stare out at the rain and think of a ship and its cargo, of the "plentifull rain . . . that continued a day or two,"[11] of thirst and frenzy. And of a story that cannot be told. I never finished reading the novel my journal reveals—I turned instead to the law: certain, objective, and predictable, it would cut through the emotions like a laser to seal off vessels oozing sadness, anger, and despair. I yield to a simple but profound curiosity—about the sea, a captain, the sailors, and a ship. About a "cargo." And the story that must tell itself.

Law and poetry both share an inexorable concern with language—the "right" use of the "right" words, phrases, or even marks of punctuation; precision of expression is the goal shared by both. In the case of the former this concern has both material and nonmaterial outcomes. A rightly worded contract, for instance, can save an individual from financial loss, or secure great financial benefits. A proper interpretation of legislation can result in an individual's physical freedom, confirmation of civil or human rights, or even death. In *Gregson v. Gilbert* the material and nonmaterial would come together in unexpected ways. An accurate interpretation of the contract of insurance, according to the owners of the *Zong*, that is, would result in great financial benefit to them: they would be paid for murdering 150 Africans. At the same time, it would mean that the deliberate drowning of 150 people was not murder, but merely the disposition of property in a time of emergency to ensure preservation of the rest of the "cargo"—a reasonable interpretation at that time given the law governing contracts of insurance. However, even if the courts had found against the owners of the *Zong* and ruled that they could not claim insurance compensation, given the law at that time, neither Captain Collingwood nor those who had helped in the massacre could be charged with murder, since what was destroyed, being property, was not capable of being murdered.[12]

> *I enter a different land, a land of language—I allow the language to lead*
> *me somewhere—don't know where, but I trust.*
> *• water of want*
> *Everything is here I tell myself—birth, death, life—murder, the law,*
> *a microcosm—a universe.*

My intent is to use the text of the legal decision as a word store; to lock myself into this particular and peculiar discursive landscape in the belief that the story of these African men, women, and children thrown overboard in an attempt to collect insurance monies, the story that can only be told by not telling, is locked in this text. In the many silences within the Silence of the text. I would lock myself in this text in the same way men, women, and children were locked in the holds of the slave ship *Zong*. But this is a story that can only be told by not telling, and how am I to not tell the story that has to be told. I return to my notes made the year before:

> *July 12, '01*
> *The only reason why we have a record is because of insurance—a record of property*
> *criteria for selection:*

- *verbs*
- *nouns, adjectives*
- *random selection that parallels the random selection of Africans*
- *it is in the text—the challenge, it leaps out*
- *the Africans are in the text*
- *the legal report is the tomb stone which speaks*
- *limitation—haiku, sonnets*
- *the limitation here is the text itself—the language comprising the record*

Language appears to be a given—we believe we have the freedom to choose any words we want to work with from the universe of words, but so much of what we work with is a given.

- *madness outside of the box of order*
- *the impulse to order there all the time*
- *grammar an ordering but a violent and necessary ordering*
- *a violent but necessary ordering*
- *there are two poems—the one i want to write and the one writing itself*
- *something underneath there but which doesn't want to spell itself out—there is an underlying current not fleshed out but there all the same*

When I start spacing out the words, there is something happening in the eye tracking the words across the page, working to pull the page and larger "meaning" together—the eye trying to order what cannot be ordered, trying to "make sense" of something, which is what it must have been like trying to understand what was happening on board the Zong—meantime there are smaller individual poems to be found in different places on the page as the lines are juxtaposed and work together.

July 21, '01
The legal text parallels a certain kind of entity—a whole, a completeness which like African life is rent and torn.
This time though I do the tearing—but always there is this movement towards trying to "make sense," make it "readable," "understandable."

- *making a whole from a fragment, or, perhaps, a fragment from a whole*
- *logic from illogic*
- *rationality from irrationality*
- *find myself trying to find reason in the language that I myself have fractured and fragmented and yet being dissatisfied when the poem becomes too comprehensible*

The ones I like best are those where the poem escapes the net of complete understanding—where the poem is shot through with glimmers of meaning.

One approach was literally to cut up the text and just pick words randomly, then I

would write them down but nothing seemed to yield—this was most similar to the activity of the random picking of African slaves—selected randomly then thrown together, hoping that something would come of it—that they would produce something. Owners did have an interest in them working together, like I do in having words work together. That working together only achieved through force. In my case, it is grammar which is the ordering mechanism, the mechanism of force.
- *am interested in them not working together—resisting that order and desire or impulse to meaning*
- *my urge to make sense must be resisted*
- *have argued that there are always at least 2 poems—the one you want to write and the other that must write itself, and this work appears to be the culmination of that because am not even using my own words. Are they ever my own words, though?*

Dramatis personae (justices and lawyers)
  Davenport
  Piggott
  Heywood
  Mansfield
  Willes
  Buller
  Lee
  Chambre

All the justices agree that the action of the ship owner was wrong—in law, that is, but not because it was murder—wanting to leave off articles, conjunctions, etc.
- *not reading text for meaning, but for something else*
- *choosing verbs and nouns—criteria for selection as Africans were selected*

To not tell the tale that must be told I employ a variety of techniques:

—I white out and black out words (is there a difference?).

—I mutilate the text as the fabric of African life and the lives of these men, women and children were mutilated.

—I murder the text, literally cut it into pieces, castrating verbs, suffocating adjectives, murdering nouns, throwing articles, prepositions, conjunctions overboard, jettisoning adverbs: I separate subject from verb, verb from object—create semantic mayhem, until my hands bloodied, from so much killing and cutting, reach into the stinking, eviscerated innards, and like some seer, sangoma,[13] or prophet who, having sacrificed an animal for signs and portents of a new life, or simply life, reads the untold story that tells itself by not telling.

Very early on I develop a need to know the names of the murdered and actually call James Walvin, author of *Black Ivory*, in England to ask him if he knew how I could locate them. "Oh no," his tone is commiserative, "they didn't keep names." I don't—cannot believe this to be true, but later on, as a result of correspondence with a colleague who is researching and writing a book on the *Zong* case,[14] I receive a copy of a sales book kept by one Thomas Case, an agent in Jamaica who did business with the owners of the *Zong*. It is typical of the records kept at that time: Purchasers are identified while Africans are reduced to the stark description of "negroe man," [*sic*] "negroe woman," or, more frequently, "ditto man," "ditto woman." There is one gloss to this description: "Negroe girl (meagre)." There are many "meagre" girls, no "meagre" boys. This description leaves me shaken—I want to weep. I leave the photocopied sheet of the ledger sitting on my old typewriter for days. I cannot approach the work for several days.

The African men, women, and children on board the *Zong* were stripped of all specificity, including their names. Their financial value, however, was recorded and preserved for insurance purposes, each being valued at 30 pounds sterling.[15]

When I return to the manuscript I find I need more working space and decide to set up another desk that allows me to turn my back on my room. There is a moment of panic: Should I be looking at all the documents related to the case, such as the trial transcripts or Granville Sharp's letter to the Court of King's Bench, with a view to using the language there as well? The text of *Gregson v. Gilbert* appears so modest, so fragile, so "meagre." I "decide against it—important to keep the limitation," I write, reminding myself that the case is the tombstone, the one public marker of the murder of those Africans on board the *Zong*, locating it in a specific time and place. It is a public moment, a textual monument marking their murder and their existence, their small histories that ended so tragically.

I fight the desire to impose meaning on the words—it is so instinctive, this need to impose meaning: this is the generating impulse of, and towards, language, isn't it—to make and, therefore, to communicate, meaning? How did they—the Africans on board the *Zong*—make meaning of what was happening to them? What meaning did they make of it and how did they make it mean? This story that must be told; that can only be told by not telling.

July 12, '02
Some—all the poems—need a great deal of space around them—as if there is too much cramping around them, as if they need to breathe . . .
  • what am I doing? Giving voice—crying out?

• for the first time am looking at breaking down the words themselves and pulling words out of them

• the words suggesting how to work with them—I look at them and certain words leap out at me, asking me to choose them; a sense at times of doing something for these hidden people, these lost kin . . . I burn incense, eyes skimming the text for phrases, words, feelings, as one would cast one's eyes over the sea looking for bodies—so much flotsam and jetsam . .

• the text is whole

• then rent

• always what is going on seems to be about water

The poems resist my attempts at meaning or coherence and, at times, I too approach the irrationality and confusion, if not madness (*madness is outside of the box of order*), of a system that could enable, encourage even, a man to drown 150 people as a way to maximize profits—the material and the nonmaterial. Or is it the immaterial? Within the boundaries established by the words and their meanings there are silences; within each silence is the poem, which is revealed only when the text is fragmented and mutilated, mirroring the fragmentation and mutilation that slavery perpetrated on Africans, their customs and ways of life.

I witness a continuation of my engagement with the idea of Silence vis-à-vis silence begun in *Looking for Livingstone* [16]: There I explored it as one would a land, becoming aware that Silence was its own language that one could read, interpret, and even speak.

July 30, '02

The poems proceed slowly—feel am getting the hang of it—the style, the rhythm. Should I do a long poem in my own voice? There is a phrase that hangs around, is always there: the ancients walk within us. A Canadian sculptor, Dawn McNutt, whose work I like uses this phrase in her catalogue. It holds me—all the ancients walk within us. It's attributed to Jung but she has been unable, after much searching, to verify this.

Dawn, too, talks of faults and fragments in her work.

The poems are about language at its most fundamental in the sense of the very basic way in which children put language together when they begin to speak, building syllable on syllable—carefully—leaving off articles: Africans want water . . .

• a sense of having to let go

• the poems demand that I let go

• several of the poems appear to be about water—why not?

• I light incense each time—in memory of

• words need a lot of space to breathe—breathing space

• and what's happening is little bits of poetry appearing within the larger poem

There is no telling this story

In its potent ability to decree that what is is not, as in a human ceasing to be and becoming an object, a thing or chattel, the law approaches the realm of magic and religion. The conversion of human into chattel becomes an act of transubstantiation the equal of the metamorphosis of the eucharistic bread and wine into the body and blood of Christ. Like a magic wand the law erases all ties—linguistic, societal, cultural, familial, parental, and spiritual; it strips the African down to the basic common denominator of man, woman, or child, albeit sometimes meagre. Without a history, name, or culture. In life but without life. Without life in life—with a story that cannot but must be told.

"*Oath moan mutter chant . . . babble curse chortle . . . ululation*": These words would in *She Tries Her Tongue; Her Silence Softly Breaks*[17] metamorphose into intelligible speech. To chart the outline of the wound. I am reminded of Lindon Barrett's argument in *Blackness and Value* that the shout was the "principal context in which black creativity occurred."[18] In *Looking for Livingstone*, the metamorphosis occurs when the lower case "silence" of the colonised becomes the fertile Silence of the Traveller, a Silence that arises from a rooting in tradition and a knowing of what the colonial script was all about. In *Zong!*, the African, transformed into a thing by the law, is re-transformed, miraculously, back into human. Through oath and through moan, through mutter, chant and babble, through babble and curse, through chortle and ululation to not-tell the story . . .

> "*The poet is a detective and the detective a poet," writes Thomas Moore,*[19] *and that's what I feel like—a detective sifting the evidence, trying to remove the veil hiding the facts.*

What did, in fact, happen on the *Zong*? Can we, some two hundred years later, ever really know? Should we? These are the questions I confront. Although presented with the "complete" text of the case, the reader does not ever know it, since the complete story does not exist. It never did. All that remains are the legal texts and documents of those who were themselves intimately connected to, and involved in, a system that permitted the murder of the Africans on board the *Zong*.

> *August 2002*
> - *poems about language—some poems just fall—fall into place*
> - *the muscle of a poem is in the verbs—found that when I was working on one with no verbs—couldn't do anything with it*
> - *muscles give shape, hold it up*
> - *some poems just seem to offer themselves up*

• am here at the desk I've put at the south wall—suddenly a piece of paper floats down, apparently from nowhere—it contains notes I had earlier made on the Bantu view of death and the afterlife of ancestors—those who have died but continue to work on behalf of the living

I deeply distrust this tool I work with—language. It is a distrust rooted in certain historical events that are all of a piece with the events that took place on the *Zong*. The language in which those events took place promulgated the non-being of African peoples, and I distrust its order, which hides disorder; its logic hiding the illogic and its rationality, which is simultaneously irrational. However, if language is to do what it must do, which is communicate, these qualities—order, logic, rationality—the rules of grammar must be present. And, as it is with language, so too with the law. Exceptions to these requirements exist in religious or spiritual communication with nonhuman forces such as gods or supra-human beings, in puns, parables, and, of course, poetry. In all these instances humans push against the boundary of language by engaging in language that often is neither rational, logical, predictable or ordered. It is sometimes even non-comprehensible, as in the religious practice of speaking in tongues, which fatally subverts the very purpose of language. Poetry comes the closest to this latter type of communication—is, indeed, rooted in it—not only in pushing against the boundaries of language, but in the need for each poet to speak in his or her own tongue. So, in *She Tries Her Tongue*, the imperative for me was to move beyond representation of what the New World experience was—even one filtered through my own imagination and knowing, for that would have meant working entirely within the order of logic, rationality, and predictability; it would have meant ordering an experience which was disordered (and cannot ever be ordered), irrational, illogical and unpredictable; it would have meant doing a second violence, this time to the memory of an already violent experience. The disorder, illogic and irrationality of the *Zong!* poems can no more tell the story than the legal report of *Gregson v. Gilbert* masquerading as order, logic, and rationality. In their very disorder and illogic is the not-telling of the story that must be told.

October 4, '02
Am stumped by some of the poems. Suddenly they stop being about language and I feel tired. Seems I was trying to put my own meaning on the words and that doesn't work. Have to let them offer themselves up. Have found a batch of rough ones at the back and they move but they move more towards the lyric and less towards language. Not sure why yet.

On their surface the poems approximate language poetry; like the language poets I question the assumed transparency of language and, therefore, employ similar strategies to reveal the hidden agendas of language. In my own work, however, the strategies signpost a multifaceted critique of the European project. Language was and is integral to this project, hence the centrality of the critique of language in my work. In the present case I use the text of the legal report almost as a painter uses paint or a sculptor stone—the material with which I work being preselected and limited. Henry Moore observed that his manner of working was to remove all extraneous material to allow the figure that was "locked" in the stone to reveal itself. It is an image that has always appealed to me, although I work with words rather than stone.

Having engaged with this idea, however, I realize that in my approach to this text I have only revealed what is commonplace, although hidden: that even when we believe we have freedom to use whatever words we wish to use, that we have the entire lexicon of English, at least those of us who are Anglophone, at our disposal, and are able to express ourselves in whatever ways we wish to (all of us who live in the so-called liberal democracies, that is), much of the language we work with is already preselected and limited, by fashion, by cultural norms—by systems that shape us such as gender and race—by what's acceptable. By order, logic, and rationality. This, indeed, is also the story that cannot be told, yet must be told.

> *October 4, '02*
> • *was one poem in which I began carving words out of other words:*
> "*defend the dead*" *is first one*
> *carving words out of names of justices and lawyers*
> *pig*
> *man*
> *port*
> *field*
> *wood*
> *bull*

The not-telling of this particular story is in the fragmentation and mutilation of the text, forcing the eye to track across the page in an attempt to wrest meaning from words gone astray. I teeter between accepting the irrationality of the event and the fundamental human impulse to make meaning from phenomena around us. The resulting abbreviated, disjunctive, almost non-sensical style of the poems demands a corresponding effort on the part of the reader to "make sense" of an event that eludes understanding, perhaps permanently. What is "it" about? What is happening? In asking those questions there are echoes here, more than two hundred years later, of what it must have been like for those Africans on board the *Zong*. "Negroes want . . . sustenance preservation rest . . .want water . . . overboard."[20] In the discomfort and disturbance created by the poetic text, I am forced to make meaning from apparently disparate elements—in so doing I implicate myself. The risk—of contamination—lies in piecing together the story that cannot be told. And since we have to work to complete the events, we all become implicated in, if not contaminated by, this activity.

The irony here is that the story is locked within the text of those individuals—members of the judiciary, one of, if not the most powerful segment of English society—who were themselves an integral part of a system that engaged in the trade in humans. A system of laws, rules, and regulations that made possible the massacre on board the *Zong*. It is a story that cannot be told; a story that in not telling must tell itself, using the language of the only publicly extant document directly bearing on these events—a legal report that is, at best, only tangentially related to the Africans on board the *Zong*.

In simultaneously censoring the activity of the reported text while conjuring the presence of excised Africans, as well as their humanity, I become both censor and magician. As censor, I function like the law whose role is to proscribe and prescribe, deciding which aspects of the text will be removed and which remain; I replicate the censorial activity of the law, which determines which facts should or should not become evidence; what is allowed into the record and what not. The fact that Africans were human could not be allowed into the legal text. Like the law, I decide what is or is not. As magician, however, I conjure the infinite(ive) of to be of the "negroes" on board the *Zong*. This is the axis on which the text of *Zong!* turns: censor and magician; the told and the untold; the telling and the un-telling of what cannot, yet must, be told. In the struggle to avoid imposing meaning, I confront the tension between the poem that I want to write and the poem that must write itself. While a concern with precision and accuracy in language is common to both law and poetry, the law uses language as a tool for ordering; in the instant case, however, I want poetry to disassemble the ordered, to create disorder and mayhem so as to release the story that cannot be told, but which, through not-telling, will tell itself.

Oct. 12, '02
  • *found these later poems a struggle—as if having to work harder to resist my meaning—more lyric . . .*

The story that cannot be told must not-tell itself in a language already contaminated, possibly irrevocably and fatally. I resist the seduction of trying to cleanse it through ordering techniques and practices, for the story must tell itself, even if it is a partial story; it must be allowed to be and not be. The half-tellings, and un-tellings force me to enter the zone of contamination to complete it; in so doing I risk being contaminated by the prescribed language of the law—by language in fact. The basic tool in the study of law is case analysis. This process requires a careful sifting of the reported case to find the kernel of the legal principle at the heart of the decision—the *ratio decidendi* or simply the *ratio*. Having isolated that, all other opinion becomes *obiter dicta*, informally referred to as *dicta*. Which is what the Africans on board the *Zong* become—*dicta*, footnotes, related to, but not, the *ratio*.

November 25, '03
Caledon, Ontario
I cannot say when I first conceive the idea but once it has taken hold I know that I
must honour it. "Defend the dead." The Africans on board the Zong must be named.
They will be ghostly footnotes floating below the text—"under water . . . a place of
consequence"

Idea at heart of the footnotes in general is acknowledgment—someone else was
here before—in Zong! footnote equals the footprint.

Footprints of the African on board the Zong.

On the "surface" the ratio of *Gregson v. Gilbert* was that "the evidence [did] not sup-
port the statement of the loss made in the declaration;"[21] in other words, given the ev-
idence presented to the court, the ship's owners had not satisfactorily proved that they
needed to "jettison their cargo," that is, murder 150 African slaves.[22] The "underwater"
ratio appears to be that the law supersedes being, that being is not a constant in time,
but can be changed by the law. The *ratio* at the heart of *Zong!*, however, is simply the
story of be-ing which cannot, but must, be told. Through not-telling. And where the
law attempts to extinguish be-ing, as happened for 400 years as part of the European
project, be-ing trumps the law every time.

Can I? Should I? Will I? Must I? I did. "Break and Enter"[23] the text to release its
anti-meaning.

Dec. 15, 2003, Tobago
Letter to CB
"The text has exploded into a universe of words."
  • have given in to the impulse to fragment the words of the text—using it as a
  sort of grand boggle game and set to trying to find words within words. The
  text—the reported case—is a matrix—a mother document. I did not come to
  the decision easily—to break the words open. For a while I feel guilt, as if I
  have broken my own rules, but that is where the impulse leads—to explode
  the words to see what other words they may contain. I devise a dictionary with
  a list of each of the 'mother' words followed by the words contained in that
  particular word—for instance, apprehension yields hen, sion, pare and pear,
  to list a few possibilities. As I put the dictionary together, little dramas appear
  to take place in the margins of the text and so the poem continues to write it-
  self, giving up its stories and resulting in four subsequent movements or books
  —I think of these poems as the flesh—the earlier 26 poems are the bones.

  The alphabet is the universe of language—all the sounds contained in each
  alphabet of letters and each letter a fragment—of the whole
  • a link between the dynamic of the text containing everything and the fundamental
  flaw that led to Africans being taken.

• women's voices surfacing in the text—which attempts to neutralize everything sud-denly references to menstruation and childbirth and rape—in contrast with the absence of women in the larger Caribbean text as it's articulated at present—and then reading the Granville Sharp's letter yesterday—24/01/04—there is reference to women, infants and children—that slows me down—something so raw about that letter—he is so much closer in time to it and it's not neutral—he is taking a side and I am so interested in how someone can be so contrary to his age

• am unable to go on when he questions how many people would have understood English when the commands were given for them to jump or throw themselves over-board—cannot read on—too much for me

It is fall 2005: I attend a talk at Hart House, University of Toronto, by a young forensic anthropologist, Clea Koff, who has written a book about working in Rwanda and Bosnia identifying the bones of the murdered.[24] It's important, she says, for bodies to be exhumed—in doing so you return dignity to the dead. What is the word for bring-ing bodies back from water? From a "liquid grave"?[25] Months later I do an Internet search for a word or phrase for bringing someone back from underwater that has as precise a meaning as the unearthing contained within the word exhume. I find words like resurrect and subaquatic but not "exaqua." Does this mean that unlike being in-terred, once you're underwater there is no retrieval—that you can never be "exhumed" from water? The gravestone or tombstone marks the spot of interment, whether of ashes or the body. What marks the spot of subaquatic death? Families need proof, Koff says—they come looking for recognizable clothing and say, "I want the bones."

I, too, want the bones.

I come—albeit slowly—to the understanding that *Zong!* is hauntological; it is a work of haunting, a wake of sorts, where the spectres of the undead make themselves present. And only in not-telling can the story be told; only in the space where it's not told—literally in the margins of the text, a sort of negative space, a space not so much of non-meaning as anti-meaning.

Our entrance to the past is through memory—either oral or written. And water. In this case saltwater. Sea water. And, as the ocean appears to be the same yet is con-stantly in motion, affected by tidal movements, so too this memory appears stationary yet is shifting always. Repetition drives the event and the memory simultaneously,[26] becoming a haunting, becoming spectral in its nature.

Haunted by "generations of skulls and spirits,"[27] I want the bones.

November 2005—Munich Airport

While waiting to make a connection, I sit and watch the flow of people and suddenly become aware that the fragment appears more precious, more beautiful than the whole, if only for its brokenness. Perhaps, the fragment allows for the imagination

to complete its missing aspects—we can talk, therefore, of the poetics of frag-
mentation.[28]

Re-reading *Specters of Marx* by Derrida has clarified some of my own thoughts and confirmed me in my earlier feelings that *Zong!* is a wake. It is a work that employs memory in the service of mourning—an act that could not be done before, as I've argued in an earlier essay about the possible and potential functions of memory.[29] Using Hamlet to interrogate the apparently defunct place and role of Marx and Marxism, Derrida asserts that we must identify the remains and localize the dead. The "work of mourning,"[30] he writes, demands clarity: that we know who the deceased is; whose grave it is; where the grave is and that the body or bodies "remain there"—in situ. This imperative for identification, this necessity to lay the bones to rest, echoes the remarks of the young forensic scientist.

I feel strongly that I need to seek "permission" to bring the stories of these murdered Africans to light—above the surface of the water—to "exaqua" them from their "liquid graves." Indeed, the stories of all the dead. And so, not knowing what this "permission" would look like or even why I feel the need, I journey to Ghana in the summer of 2006. While there I visit a traditional shrine close to one of the slave ports in the homeland of the Ewe people, and meet with the elders and the priest of the shrine. In preparation for this meeting I must dress in cloth, I am told—traditional African cloth, and so I am wrapped by an older woman from head to toe in a beautifully patterned fabric. I remember it as brown and gold. At the shrine I make the traditional offering of Schnapps to the priest and, following the example of the elders, touch my forehead to the ground, after which, and through a translator, we talk of the *Zong*. Of its presence in my life and what it means. None of my ancestors could have been among those thrown overboard, one elder offers. If that were the case, he continues, I would not be there. I am startled. I stare at him, a compact man with the face of a scholar or thinker. A man whose face I recognize—perhaps it is the kindness I see there—although I have never met him before. I have never entertained the thought that I may have had a personal connection to the *Zong*, nor have I ever sought to understand why this story has chosen me. Fundamentally, I don't think it matters, but his comment is still disconcerting. A full year later, on recounting the comment to my daughter, she responds to his comment:" Only if those who were thrown overboard left no offspring on board the *Zong*." Once again I am startled. Again not because I want or even care to link myself to the *Zong*. I am startled at how we, that old man and I, so easily forgot the "meagre" ones—the children. Also, I believe that he, not knowing the story, was unaware that only some of the African slaves were drowned. Before leaving I make an offering to the shrine and to all those lost souls on board the *Zong*.

My flight is routed through London; I plan to spend a few days there so that I can once again visit Liverpool and its Merseyside Maritime Museum in which there is a permanent exhibit on transatlantic slavery. On my way to England from Ghana via Amsterdam, high up above the earth I am suddenly aware of why I am going to Liverpool, home of the Gregsons, Gilberts, and, not to mention, the good Captain Luke Collingwood. There will be no priests to visit, no one to talk to about a ship and its cargo—a ship that had set sail from that very port. I do know, however, that I have to acknowledge the existence of those Europeans on board the *Zong*, those who like many Africans sickened and died, as well as those who were involved in the murder of the Africans, and thus in the murder of their own souls. And so, I go down to the old port in Merseyside, Liverpool. Hundreds of slave-ships would have set off from this port for what was then known as the Gold Coast of Africa, their holds filled with all manner of things—cloth, guns, beads—to trade. For people. For men, women, and children who would, in turn, be stuffed—things—in the same hold for what would for them be a one way journey to death—living or real. I go down to the water in Merseyside, Liverpool, and pour a libation of spirits for the lost souls on board the *Zong*. All the souls. The approach to the water is mossy and slippery and on my way back from pouring the spirits I fall flat on my ass. I am embarrassed, wondering if anyone has seen me fall and whether the fall means the pleasure or displeasure on the part of the Ancestors.

For the longest while the manuscript weighs heavily: having exploded the words, having scooped the stories out of the magma of the text, the work appears too long and the apparent lyric form and approach of this second part of the book—the four movements—troubles me somewhat, although I accept it. In the fall of 2006, however, having returned from Ghana, and in a farmhouse in the Ontario countryside, the poem finds its own form, its own voice: It suggests something about the relational—every word or word cluster is seeking a space directly above within which to fit itself and in so doing falls into relation with others either above, below, or laterally. This is the governing principle and adds a strongly visual quality to the work.

Zong! bears witness to the "resurfacing of the drowned and the oppressed"[31] and transforms the desiccated, legal report into a cacophony of voices—wails, cries, moans, and shouts that had earlier been banned from the text. I recall hearing a radio interview with Gavin Bryars, composer of *The Sinking, the Titanic*, in which he discusses the idea of sound never ceasing within water, an idea that he suggests Marconi believed, since water is a much more "sound-efficient medium"[32] than air. I have often since wondered whether the sounds of those murdered Africans continue to resound and echo underwater. In the bone beds of the sea.

Our entrance to the past is through memory. And water. It is happening always—repeating always, the repetition becoming a haunting. Do they, the sounds, the cries, the shouts of those thrown overboard from the *Zong* repeat themselves over and over until they rise from the ocean floor to resurface in *Zong!*? It is a question that haunts me. As do the "generations of skulls and spirits."[33] The spirit in the text and of the text is at work. Working against meaning, working for meaning, working in and out of meaning.

It came upon me one day that the fugue—in both meanings of the word—was a frame through which I could understand *Zong!* In the musical sense of the word, *Zong!* is a counterpointed, fugal antinarrative in which several strands are simultaneously at work. In the classic, fugal form the theme is stated then reiterated in second, third, and subsequent voices. In a similar fashion *Zong!* is a sustained repetition or reiteration of various themes, phrases and voices, albeit fragmented. Interestingly enough, one of the pieces of music that sustained the "writing" of this work was *Spem in Alium,* a forty- voice motet by Thomas Tallis employing five choirs of eight voices. Antiphonal in nature, it prefigures in its form and texture the later fugue.[34]

The fugue has, however, another darker meaning, referring to a state of amnesia in which the individual, his or her subjectivity having been destroyed, becomes alienated from him- or herself. It is a state that can be as brief as a few hours or as lengthy as several years.[35] In its erasure and forgetting of the be-ing and humanity of the Africans on board the *Zong,* the legal text of *Gregson v. Gilbert* becomes a representation of the fugal state of amnesia, serving as a mechanism for erasure and alienation. Further, in my fragmenting the text and re-writing it through *Zong!,* or rather over it, thereby essentially erasing it, the original text becomes a fugal palimpsest through which *Zong!* is allowed to heal the original text of its fugal amnesia.

Describing one of his recent installations—*Inconsolable Memories*[36]—the visual artist Stan Douglas characterizes the work as a recombinant narrative, a technique in which he loops several different narrative strands from the present, past, and future to retell a 1968 Cuban film.[37] The "video or film works repeat looped scenes in an ever-changing order, switch sound tracks from one to another and generally thwart our reflective need for linear narrative."[38] I am excited by, and recognize, the parallels with the for-mal ideas in *Zong!* To my mind, however, *Zong!* is not so much a recombinant narrative as a recombinant antinarrative. The story that can't ever be told.

The parallels go further: In an essay titled "Fugal Encryptions," Philip Monk, cur-ator of *Inconsolable Memories*, argues that Douglas employs strategies that succeed in apparently "absolving" his work of "authorial intention."[39] In allowing myself to sur-render to the text—silences and all—and allowing the fragmented words to speak to the stories locked in the text, I, too, have found myself "absolved" of "authorial in-tention." So much so that even claiming to author the text through my own name is challenged by the way the text has shaped itself. The way it "untells" itself.

One of the strongest "voices" in the *Zong!* text is that of someone who appears to be white, male, and European. Had I approached this "story" in the manner of want-ing to write the story *about* the *Zong* and the events surrounding its fateful journey, I would not have chosen a white, male, European voice as one of the primary voices in this work. My "authorial intention" would have impelled me toward other voices. And for very good reason. This realization, however, presents me with a powerful example of how our language—in the wider sense of that word—is often, as I wrote earlier here, preselected for us, simply by virtue of who we understand ourselves to be, and where we allow ourselves to be placed. And, by refusing the risk of allowing ourselves to be absolved of authorial intention, we escape an understanding that we are at least one and the Other. And the Other. And the Other. That in this post post-modern world we are, indeed, multiple and "many-voiced."[40]

Monk's use of the word "absolve" is intriguing, given its connection with the idea of freeing from debt, blame, obligation, or guilt. Within the moral framework of *Zong!*, however, I find it an appropriate word in that it points to a relation and relationship, between past, present, and future generations; it speaks to a relation and relationship of debt or obligation of spirit owed by later to earlier generations. And I understand now how this, in turn, relates to the organizing principle of relationship used in *Zong!* mentioned earlier.

As the work shapes itself after my return from Africa—in the books or movements that develop after the first twenty-six poems—words rearrange themselves in odd and bizarre combinations: at times the result appears the verbal equivalent of the African American dance style "crumping,"[41] in which the body is contorted and twisted into intense positions and meanings that often appear beyond human comprehension. At times it feels as if I am getting my revenge on "this/fuck-mother motherfuckin language"[42] of the colonizer—the way the text forces you—me—to read differently, bringing chaos into the language or, perhaps more accurately, revealing the chaos that is already there.

The stories on board the *Zong* that comprise *Zong!* are jammed together—"crumped"—so that the ordering of grammar, the ordering that is the impulse of empire is subverted. Clusters of words sometimes have meaning, often do not—words are broken into and open to make non-sense or no sense at all, which, in turn, becomes a code for another submerged meaning. Words break into sound, return to their initial and originary phonic sound—grunts, plosives, labials—is this, perhaps, how language might have sounded at the beginning of time?

There are times in the final book, *Ferrum*, when I feel as if I am writing a code and, oddly enough, for the very first time since writing chose me, I feel that I *do* have a language—this language of grunt and groan, of moan and stutter—this language of pure sound fragmented and broken by history. This language of the limp and the wound. Of the fragment. And, in its fragmentation and brokenness the fragment becomes mine. Becomes me. Is me. The ultimate question on board the *Zong* is what happened? Could it be that language happened? The same letters in the same order mean different things in different languages: ague and *ague*—the first English, the second Yoruba. The former meaning bodily shaking in illness, the latter, to fast. Take a letter away and a new word in a different language is born. Add a letter and the word loses meaning. The loss of language and meaning on board the *Zong* levels everyone to a place where there is, at times, no distinction between languages—everyone, European and African alike, has reverted, it appears, to a state of pre-literacy.

> *How do I read a work like this? This is the same question I faced after writing*
> She Tries . . .

One of the names that surfaces in the text of *Zong!* is Dido and along with it a cluster of images about the historical Dido and her founding the city of Carthage. A couple of years later, as I browse a bookstore in Toronto I come upon Simon Schama's *Rough Crossings*,[43] a work about Britain, the slave trade, and the American revolution. He recounts the story of the *Zong*, but what is startling is the history he reveals about Lord Mansfield, Chief Justice of England, who, as mentioned earlier, presided at the appeal in *Gregson v. Gilbert*. His nephew, Captain John Lindsay, was a sea captain who had captured a Spanish slaving vessel and, it appears, fathered a daughter with an African woman on board that ship—the name of that child was Dido Elizabeth Belle Lindsay. Dido grew up in her great uncle's, Lord Mansfield's, home, where, it appears, she was treated as a relative, albeit one of lesser standing.[44] The well-known English painter Johan Zoffany was commissioned to paint a portrait of her and her cousin, Lady Elizabeth Murray, which is now on display at Scone Palace in Scotland. The details of the relationship between Captain Lindsay and Dido's mother are not recounted. Was she raped? Was there ever, in fact, a relationship? Why was the child brought to England and allowed to reside with Lord Mansfield? This link between a name or word that surfaced in the text and actual events is one of the most startling of serendipitous events that have "marked" the making of *Zong!*

Another was computer related: Having completed the first draft of one section I attempt to print it; the laser printer for no apparent reason prints the first two or three pages superimposed on each other—crumped, so to speak—so that the page becomes a dense landscape of text. The subsequent pages are, however, printed as they should be. With the beginning of each movement of the second part of the book—*Sal, Ventus, Ratio*, and *Ferrum*—the same thing happens. I have never been able to find a reason for it and my printer has not since done that with anything else I have written.

I now think of the poems that come after the first twenty-six as a translation of the opacity of those early poems—a translation that, like all good translations, has a life of its own. Together, *Os, Sal, Ventus, Ratio*, and *Ferrum*[45] comprise the movements of *Zong!*, the story that must be told that cannot be told, which in turn becomes a metaphor for slavery—*the* story that simultaneously cannot be told, must be told, and will never be told.

The descendants of that experience appear creatures of the word, apparently brought into ontological being by fiat and by law. The law it was that said we were. Or were not. The fundamental resistance to this, whether or not it was being manifested in the many, many instances of insurrection, was the belief and knowledge that we—the creatures of fiat and law—always knew we existed outside of the law—that law—and that our be-ing was prior in time to fiat, law and word. Which converted us to property: *"pig port field wood bull negroe."* It is a painful irony that today so many of us continue to live, albeit in an entirely different way, either outside of the law, or literally imprisoned within it. Unable to not-tell the story that must be told.

The continued exclusion of African Americans (I would say New World Africans) from systems of value, Lindon Barrett argues, creates a need to "pursue novel or original access to meaning, voice, value and authority."[46] In its cacophonous representation of the babel that was the *Zong*, *Zong!* attempts and tempts just such access to meaning.

Many is the time in the writing of this essay when my fingers would hit an S rather than a Z in typing *Zong*. Song and Zong: with the exception of one letter the two words are identical; if said quickly enough they sound the same. In the title poem of *She Tries Her Tongue* I write:

> *When silence is*
> *Abdication of word tongue and lip*
> *Ashes of once in what was*
> *. . . Silence*
> *Song Word Speech*
> *Might I . . . like Philomela . . . sing*
>
> > *continue*
> >
> > > *over*
> > >
> > > > *into*
>
> *. . . pure utterance*[47]

Why the exclamation mark after *Zong!*? *Zong!* is chant! Shout! And ululation! *Zong!* is moan! Mutter! Howl! And shriek! *Zong!* is "pure utterance." *Zong!* is Song! And Song is what has kept the soul of the African intact when they "want(ed) water . . . sustenance . . . preservation."[48] *Zong!* is the Song of the untold story; it cannot be told yet must be told, but only through its un-telling.

NOTES

1. The name of the ship was the *Zorg*, meaning "care" in Dutch. An error was made when the name was repainted.

2. The ship left from the island of São Tomé off the coast of Gabon.

3. *Gregson v. Gilbert*, 3 Dougl. 233. The case mentions 150 slaves killed. James Walvin in *Black Ivory*, 131, others 130 and 132. The exact number of African slaves murdered remains a slippery signifier of what was undoubtedly a massacre.

4. *Substance of the Debate on a Resolution for Abolishing the Slave Trade* (London, 1806) pp. 178-9.

5. The most famous of these cases, the Somerset case, established the precedent that no one could be captured in England and taken away to be sold. Despite the best efforts of Lord Mansfield to avoid proclaiming that slavery was illegal in England, the case was quickly interpreted as establishing the law that slavery could not exist in England.

6. James Walvin, *Black Ivory* (HarperCollins Publishers, London, England, 1992) p. 16.

7. *Ibid*, p. 19.

8. One of the early drafts of the manuscript.

9. Ivan Illich, "The Corruption of Christianity," *Ideas*, CBC Radio One.

10. Bradley Crawford, Marvin G. Baer, Robert T. Donald, and James A. Rendall, eds., *Cases on the Canadian Law of Insurance* (Carswell Company Ltd, Toronto, Canada, 1971) p. 391.

11. See earlier: *Gregson v. Gilbert*.

12. The abolitionist Granville Sharp did try, unsuccessfully, to get murder charges laid against those involved in the massacre.

13. *Sangoma* is a Zulu word meaning healer of both physical and spiritual ailments.

14. Ian Baucom, *Specters of the Atlantic* (Duke University Press, Durham, North Carolina, 2005).

15. Granville Sharp, *Memoirs of Granville Sharp*, Prince Hoare, ed. (Henry Colburn and Co., London, 1820) pp. 242-244. In his letter to Lords of the Admiralty, Sharp challenged the sum of 30 pounds sterling, since women and children were assigned a lesser value.

16. *Looking for Livingstone: An Odyssey of Silence* (Mercury Publishers, Toronto, 1991).

17. m. nourbeSe philip, *She Tries Her Tongue; Her Silence Softly Breaks* (Poui Publications, Toronto, Ontario, 2006).

18. Lindon Barrett, *Blackness and Value* (Cambridge University Press, Cambridge, England, 1999).

19. Thomas Moore, *Original Soul* (HarperCollins Publishers, New York, 2000).

20. Excerpts from *Zong!*

21. See earlier: *Gregson v. Gilbert*.

22. There was evidence, for instance, that the captain had not attempted to ration the water they had on board before deciding to drown the Africans on board.

23. A charge under the Criminal Code of Canada.

24. Clea Koff, *The Bone Woman* (Alfred A. Knopf Canada, Toronto, 2004).

25. Elicia Brown Lathon, Ph.D. dissertation, "I Cried Out and None but Jesus Heard" (Louisiana State University and Agricultural and Mechanical College, 2005).

26. The events surrounding the *Zong* have long been the focus of artistic attention. The English painter J.M.W. Turner's 1840 painting, *Slavers throwing overboard the dead and the dying, Typhon Coming On*, was inspired by the event; so too was the novel *Feeding the Ghosts* by British Guyanese poet and novelist Fred D'Aguiar (Ecco, Hopewell, New Jersey, 1999). Marina Warner has also explored the event in an online essay titled "Indigo, Mapping the Waters." Ian Baucom argues in *Specters of the Atlantic* that the continued

witnessing of the *Zong* atrocity by writers and artists points to an "order of historical time" that does not so much pass as "accumulate."

27. Jacques Derrida, *Specters of Marx* (Routledge, New York, 1991) p. 9.

28. "Fugues and Fragments" in the online journal *Anthurium*, vol. 3, no. 2, Fall 2005. http://scholar.library.miami.edu/anthurium/volume_3/issue_2/philip-fugues.htm.

29. m. nourbeSe philip, "In the Matter of Memory . . . ," *Fertile Ground: Memories & Visions*, Kalamuya Salaam and Kysha N. Brown, eds. (Runngate Press, New Orleans, 1996).

30. Derrida, p. 9.

31. Poet Maureen Harris in talk at Influency, Continuing Ed., University of Toronto, December 2006.

32. Gavin Bryars, *The Sinking, The Titanic* (Polygram Group, Markham, Canada, 1994).

33. Derrida, p. 9.

34. There were certain pieces of music I played often, at times obsessively, that seemed to accompany this work. Oddly enough, Van Morrison's *Endless Days of Summer* conveyed a sense of loss of something brief, beautiful, and fleeting. So did Ali Farka Touré's *Hawa Dolo*. The simplicity and lyricism of the songs of Kenyan Luo musician Ayub Ogada recalled a memory of what might have been lost to those on board the *Zong*.

35. The Southern writer Walker Percy has explored this state in many of his novels. *Percyscapes* (Louisiana State University Press, Baton Rouge, 1999) by Robert W. Rudnicki is a helpful exploration and analysis of how the condition has been treated in literature. He includes Ralph Ellison's *Invisible Man* among novels dealing with this state.

36. Stan Douglas, *Inconsolable Memories* (York University, Toronto, 2006).

37. *Memorias del Subdesarrollo* [*Memories of Underdevelopment*], Tomás Gutiérrez Alea, director (Cuba, 97 mins., 1968).

38. Kevin Temple, "Stan Douglas," *NOW* (April 2006, vol. 25, no. 33) pp. 13-19.

39. Cindy Richmond and Scott Watson, eds., *Inconsolable Memories: Stan Douglas*, Joslyn Art Museum, Omaha, Nebraska and the Morris and Helen Belkin Art Gallery, Vancouver, British Columbia, 2005.

40. "She the many-voiced one of one voice," from "And Over Every Land and Sea" from *She Tries Her Tongue*, p. 10.

41. Crumping originated in the inner city areas of Los Angeles. It is a visceral, explosive, and expressive type of dance style that incorporates tribal and hip hop styles.

42. From "Testimony Stoops to Mother Tongue," *She Tries Her Tongue*, p. 53.

43. Simon Schama, *Rough Crossings* (Viking Canada, Toronto, 2005).

44. Dido resided with Lord Mansfield and his wife from the age of five. It appears she was raised as a lady within the family, albeit one of lesser status. It is unknown what, if any, impact Lord Mansfield's intimate contact with his mixed-race niece may have had on his views of slavery.

45. I chose Latin to emphasize the connection with the law, which is steeped in Latin expressions, and, also to reference the fact that Latin was the father tongue in Europe.

46. Barrett, p. 81.

47. *She Tries Her Tongue*, p. 98.

48. Excerpted from *Zong!*

Gregson v. Gilbert

GREGSON *v.* GILBERT. Thursday, 22d May, 1783. Where the captain of a slaveship mistook Hisaniola for Jamaica, whereby the voyage being retarded, and the water falling short, several of the slaves died for want of water, and others were thrown overboard, it was held that these facts did not support a statement in the declaration, that by the perils of the seas, and contrary winds and currents, the ship was retarded in her voyage, and by reason thereof so much of the water on board was spent, that some of the negroes died for want of sustenance, and others were thrown overboard for the preservation of the rest.

This was an action on a policy of insurance, to recover the value of certain slaves thrown overboard for want of water. The declaration stated, that by the perils of the seas, and contrary currents and other misfortunes, the ship was rendered foul and leaky, and was retarded in her voyage; and, by reason thereof, so much of the water on board the said ship, for her said voyage, was spent on board the said ship: that before her arrival at Jamaica, to wit, on, &c. a sufficient quantity of water did not remain on board the said ship for preserving the lives of the master and mariners belonging to the said ship, and of the negro slaves on board, for the residue of the said voyage; by reason whereof, during the said voyage, and before the arrival of the said ship at Jamaica — to wit, on, &c. and on divers days between that day and the arrival of the said ship at Jamaica — sixty negroes died for want of water for sustenance; and forty others, for want of water for sustenance, and through thirst and frenzy thereby occasioned, threw themselves into the sea and were drowned; and the master and mariners, for the preservation of their own lives, and the lives of the rest of the negroes, which for want of water they could not otherwise preserve, were obliged to throw overboard 150 other negroes. The facts, at the trial, appeared to be, that the ship on board of which the negroes who were the subject of this policy were, on her voyage from the coast of Guinea to Jamaica, by mistake got to leeward of that island, by mistaking it for Hispaniola, which induced the captain to bear away to leeward of it, and brought the vessel to one day's water before the mistake was discovered, when they were a month's voyage from the island, against winds and currents, in consequence of which the negroes were thrown [233] overboard. A verdict having been found for the plaintiff, a rule for a new trial was obtained on the grounds that a sufficient necessity did not exist for throwing the negroes overboard, and also that the loss was not within the terms of the policy.

Davenport, Pigott, and Heywood, in support of the rule. — There appeared in evidence no sufficient necessity to justify the captain and crew in throwing the negroes overboard. The last necessity only could authorize such a measure; and it appears, that at the time when the first slaves were thrown overboard, there were three butts of good water, and two and a half of sour water, on board. At this time, therefore, there was only an apprehended necessity, which was not sufficient. Soon afterwards the rains came on, which furnished water for eleven days, notwithstanding which more of the negroes were thrown overboard. At all events the loss arose not from the perils of the seas, but from the negligence or ignorance of the captain, for which the owners, and not the insurers, are liable. The ship sailed from Africa without sufficient water, for the casks were found to be less than was supposed. She passed Tobago without touching, though she might have made that and other islands. The declaration states, that by perils of the seas, and contrary currents and other misfortunes, the ship was rendered foul and leaky, and was retarded in her voyage; but no evidence was given that the perils of the seas reduced them to this necessity. The truth was, that finding they should have a bad market for their slaves, they took these means of transferring the loss from the owners to the underwriters. Many instances have occurred of slaves dying for want of provisions, but no attempt was ever made to bring such a loss within the policy. There is no instance in which the mortality of slaves falls upon the underwriters, except in the cases of perils of the seas and of enemies.

Lee, S.-G., and Chambre, contra. — It has been decided, whether wisely or unwisely is not now the question, that a portion of our fellow-creatures may become the subject of property. This, therefore, was a throwing overboard of goods, and of part to save the residue. The question is, first, whether any necessity existed for that act. The voyage was eighteen weeks instead of six, and that in consequence of contrary winds and calms. It was impossible to regain the island of Jamaica in less than three weeks; but it is said that [234] other islands might have been reached. This is said from the maps, and is contradicted by the evidence. It is also said that a supply of water might have been obtained at Tobago; but at that place there was sufficient for the voyage to Jamaica if the subsequent mistake had not occurred. With regard to that mistake, it appeared that the currents were stronger than usual. The apprehension of necessity under which the first negroes were thrown overboard was justified by the result. The crew themselves suffered so severely, that seven out of seventeen died after their arrival at Jamaica. There was no evidence, as stated on the other side, of any negroes being thrown overboard after the rains. Nor was it the fact that the slaves were destroyed in order to throw the loss on the underwriters. Forty or fifty of the negroes were suffered to die, and thirty were lying dead when the vessel arrived at Jamaica. But another ground has been taken, and it is said that this is not a loss within the policy. It is stated in the declaration that the ship was retarded by perils of the seas, and contrary winds and currents, and other misfortunes, &c. whereby the negroes died for want of sustenance, &c. Every particular circumstance of this averment need not be proved. In an indictment for murder it is not necessary to prove each particular circumstance. Here it sufficiently appears that the loss was primarily caused by the perils of the seas.

Lord Mansfield. — This is a very uncommon case, and deserves a reconsideration. There is great weight in the objection, that the evidence does not suppost the statement of the loss made in the declaration. There is no evidence of the ship being foul and leaky, and that certainly was not the cause of the delay. There is weight, also, in the circumstance of the throwing overboard of the negroes after the rain (if the fact be so), for which, upon the evidence, there appears to have been no necessity. There should, on the ground of reconsideration only, be a new trial, on the payment of costs.

Willes, Justice, of the same opinion.

Buller, Justice. — The cause of the delay, as proved, is not the same as that stated in the declaration. The argument drawn from the law respecting indictments for murder does not apply. There the substance of the indictment is proved, though the instrument with which the crime was effected be different from that laid. It would be dangerous [235] to suffer the plaintiff to recover on a peril not stated in the declaration, because it would not appear on the record not to have been within the policy, and the defendant would have no remedy. Suppose the law clear, that a loss happening by the negligence of the captain does not discharge the underwriters, yet upon this declaration the defendant could not raise that point.

Rule absolute on payment of costs.

M. NOURBESE PHILIP was born on the island of Tobago in the "huddled hunch-backed hills" of Woodlands, Moriah, where the blue of sky and ocean often appears as one. She studied at the University of the West Indies, Mona, Jamaica, and took graduate degrees in political science and law at Western University, London, Ontario. She practised law for seven years in Toronto, where she still lives. Her first collection of poetry, *Thorns*, was published in 1980. A further four books of poetry have followed, including the seminal *She Tries Her Tongue; Her Silence Softly Breaks* and *Looking for Livingstone: An Odyssey of Silence*.

Her published fiction includes the young-adult novel *Harriet's Daughter*, a now-classic work that navigates the adolescent friendship between two girls of Caribbean background living in Toronto, while her dramatic work includes *Coups and Calypsos*, produced in both London and Toronto in 1996.

Her essay collections, including her most recent, *BlanK*, are in the tradition of the socially and politically engaged poets, novelists, and artists of the Caribbean. Alongside her poetry, they articulate a powerful and decades-long engagement with issues generated by the destructive legacies of colonialism in both the Caribbean and Canada, even as they display a lifelong concern with the possibilities afforded by language to interrogate and remake these legacies.

Zong! As told to the author by Setaey Adamu Boateng, first published in the US and Canada in 2008, takes its title and subject from the massacre on board the *Zong* slave ship in 1781, when the captain ordered that some 150 enslaved Africans be thrown overboard to their deaths so that the ship's owners could claim insurance monies. Relying entirely on the words of the legal decision *Gregson v. Gilbert*, the only extant public document related to the massacre, *Zong!* excavates the legal text to find the stories of those on board the *Zong*—the stories that can't be told, yet must be told, and which can only be told by not-telling.

philip has received fellowships from the Guggenheim and Rockefeller Foundations, as well as numerous awards from the Ontario Arts Council and the Canada Council for the Arts. Among her literary awards are the Casa de las Américas Prize for Literature, the PEN/Nabokov Award for International Literature, and the Canada Council for the Arts Molson Prize for outstanding achievement. She was the Spring 2023 Bain-Swigget Chair in Poetry at Princeton University. In 2024, she received a Windham Campbell Prize.

KATHERINE MCKITTRICK is Canada Research Chair in Black Studies and professor in gender studies at Queen's University, Ontario. Her writings include *Demonic Grounds: Black Women and the Cartographies of Struggle* (2006) and *Dear Science and Other Stories* (2020).

SAIDIYA HARTMAN is the author of *Scenes of Subjection: Terror, Slavery, and Self-Making in Nineteenth-Century America* (1997); *Lose Your Mother: A Journey Along the Atlantic Slave Route* (2007), and *Wayward Lives, Beautiful Experiments: Intimate Histories of Social Upheaval* (2019), which received the National Book Critics Circle Award, the Publishing Triangle Judy Grahn Award, the Mary Nickliss Prize for Women and Gender History, and the Lionel Trilling Book Award. She is a MacArthur fellow and a professor at Columbia University.

Graywolf Press publishes risk-taking, visionary writers who transform culture through literature. As a nonprofit organization, Graywolf relies on the generous support of its donors to bring books like this one into the world.

This publication is made possible, in part, by the voters of Minnesota through a Minnesota State Arts Board Operating Support grant, thanks to a legislative appropriation from the arts and cultural heritage fund. Significant support has also been provided by other generous contributions from foundations, corporations, and individuals. To these supporters we offer our heartfelt thanks.

To learn more about Graywolf's books and authors or make a tax-deductible donation, please visit www.graywolfpress.org.

The text of *Zong!* is set in Clifford.
Manufactured by Sheridan on acid-free,
30 percent postconsumer wastepaper.